UNLOCK YOUR DESTINY WITH NUMEROLOGY

Uncover Self-Respect, Enhance Decision-Making, Reduce Stress, and Get Holistic Empowerment

DR. ARUN KUMAAR KHANDA
https://arunkumarrk.com

YOUR FREE GIFT

As a token of my gratitude for taking out time to read my book, I would like to offer you a free gift. Click the below link or scan the QR code to download your free eBook PDF

https//arunkumarkhanda.ck.page/00c46 de54c

Acknowledgments

In my journey as an author, I have been blessed with support that has significantly contributed to my success. I am deeply grateful to my mentor and bestselling author, Mr. Som Bathla, for his mentorship, motivation, and guidance in writing, self-publishing, and launching my books, which has been crucial on my path to becoming an author-entrepreneur.

I also extend my heartfelt thanks to my author community, especially to Sooraj Achar, a bestselling author himself, for his timely technical support, encouragement, and invaluable advice, which have made my work much easier.

My gratitude goes out to my readers for their unwavering support. I am also thankful for this incredible platform that provides authors with the resources needed to transform the lives of millions.

Thank you all for being a part of this journey. Readers can connect with me at akkhanda9@gmail.com.

Sincerely,

Arun Kumaar Khanda

MY BEST-SELLING BOOKS

AWAKENING THE SOUL SERIES

1. <u>The Path to God Consciousness</u>

2. <u>Divine Threads: Unravelling the Origins of Religious Beliefs</u>

3. <u>Maya Unveiled: Journey from Illusion to Reality</u>

4. <u>A Journey to Self-Discovery</u>

SUCCESS AND TRANSFORMATION SERIES

1. <u>Crush Your Goals</u>

2. <u>Growth Mindset Blueprint</u>

3. <u>Conquer Your Limiting Beliefs</u>

4. <u>The Art of Selective Attention</u>

5. <u>The Art of Anger Management</u>

6. <u>Unlock the Power of Positive Thinking.</u>

7. Optimistic Mindset

PREFACE

Welcome to **"Unlock Your Destiny with Numerology."** This book is designed to guide you through the fascinating world of numerology, which can help you uncover the secrets that numbers hold about your life and destiny.

Numerology is an ancient practice that has intrigued people for centuries. It's based on the idea that numbers are not just symbols for counting but hold deeper meanings and influences over our lives. In this book, you'll discover how to interpret these numbers to gain insights into your personality, relationships, and life path.

We begin with an introduction to numerology, providing a broad overview of what it is and why it's so powerful. From there, we dive into its rich history and the different systems used around the world. You'll learn about the Lo-Shu Grid, the central point of numerology, and how it can reveal hidden aspects of your character.

As we move forward, we'll explore practical applications of numerology, such as its use in lotteries and the unique concept of the Numeroscope. We'll also discuss the ancient principles that influence our lives, helping you understand how numbers can enhance your relationships and interactions.

You'll learn which numbers bring luck and which may pose challenges, giving you the tools to overcome life's ups and downs more effectively. By understanding the detailed characteristics of numbers, you'll gain deeper insights into your personality traits and life paths.

We will also explore the combinations of numbers to understand their dynamics better. The significance of the Kua Number and its impact on your environment and well-being will be covered, helping you create harmony in your surroundings. Finally, we'll discuss the Master Destiny Number and the Karmic Number, and their role in shaping your life's purpose.

"UNLOCK YOUR DESTINY WITH NUMEROLOGY" is more than just a guide—it's a journey of self-discovery. Whether you're seeking personal growth, improved relationships, or a deeper understanding of the universe, numerology offers a unique and powerful pathway.

I invite you to join me on this journey. May the knowledge you gain from this book lead you to a life of greater clarity, harmony, and fulfillment. Thank you for choosing to explore the world of numerology with me.

Author

★ ● ✪ ● ★

KEY TAKEAWAYS

Chapter:1

1. The Universal Language of Numbers

Numerology is based on the belief that numbers are the language of the universe. Just as Hans Decoz mentioned, numbers help us understand the deeper meanings of our lives. From the moment we are born, numbers play a significant role in every aspect of our existence—from our date of birth to our daily interactions.

2. The Influence of Numbers on Our Lives

Numbers are not just random figures; they are believed to carry specific vibrations and energies. In numerology, numbers from 1 to 9 are associated with different planets and have unique influences on our lives. Understanding these influences can provide insights into our personality, strengths, and challenges.

3. The Significance of Your Date of Birth

Your date of birth holds the key to your unique qualities and life path. It's more than just a date; it's a blueprint that can guide you toward understanding yourself better and unlocking your potential. Each combination of numbers in your birth chart can reveal your life's direction and the lessons you are meant to learn.

4. Overcoming Challenges with Numerology

Numerology can identify missing numbers in your birth chart, which may indicate areas where you might face challenges. However, the good news is that every problem has a solution. By understanding the gaps, you can work toward overcoming them and enhancing your strengths.

5. Empowering Yourself and Others

This book aims to teach you the fundamentals of numerology, enabling you to calculate key numbers like Moolanka and Bhagyanka. With this knowledge, you can not only improve your own life but also assist others in making better decisions and achieving success. Whether as a profession or a tool for personal growth, numerology can be a transformative journey.

Chapter:2

1. The Ancient Roots of Numerology

Numerology's origins are deeply rooted in ancient civilizations like Mesopotamia, Egypt, China, India, and Greece. These cultures believed that numbers held hidden meanings and used them for divination and understanding the universe. Pythagoras, often considered the "father of numerology," emphasized the significance of numbers in explaining the cosmos.

2. Diverse Types of Numerology

There are several types of numerology practiced around the world, including Chinese, Vedic, Cheiro, Chaldean, Pythagorean, and Western numerology. Each system has its unique approach and methodology, offering various perspectives on how numbers influence our lives. For example, Vedic numerology integrates planetary influences and karma, while Cheiro numerology is renowned for its name-correction techniques.

3. The Magical Lo-Shu Grid

The Lo-Shu Grid, a central concept in Chinese numerology, is a 3x3 magic square where the sum of the numbers in each row, column, and diagonal equals 15. This grid, also known as the Laxmi Yantra in India, is believed to hold the secrets to understanding one's destiny and character traits.

4. The Role of Numbers in Shaping Our Lives

Numerology suggests that numbers influence various aspects of our lives, including our success, relationships, health, and more. By understanding the numbers in our birth chart, we can gain insights into our strengths and weaknesses. This knowledge can help us make informed decisions and potentially transform our lives.

5. Empowerment Through Numerology

Learning numerology offers a path to self-discovery and empowerment. It can provide valuable guidance on how to overcome life's challenges and capitalize on opportunities. Whether you're interested in numerology for personal growth or as a profession, it offers a fascinating way to explore the deeper meanings behind the numbers that shape our existence.

Chapter:3

1. Understanding Lotteries in Numerology

In numerology, "lotteries" refer to the potential life outcomes and opportunities revealed by analyzing your date of birth. Each person has three key numbers: the Moolanka (Psychic Number), Bhagyanka (Destiny Number or Life Path Number), and Kua Number. These numbers provide insight into different aspects of your life.

2. Calculating the Moolanka

The Moolanka is determined by the day of your birth. If it's a double-digit number, you add the digits together to get a single digit. For example, if you were born on the 13th, your Moolanka is 4 (1+3=4).

3. Finding the Bhagyanka

The Bhagyanka is calculated by adding together all the digits in your date of birth. For instance, if your birth date is 13.08.1967, your Bhagyanka is 7 (1+3+8+1+9+6+7=35, 3+5=7).

4. Determining the Kua Number

The Kua Number varies based on gender. For males, subtract the single-digit sum of your birth year from 11. For females, add 4 to this sum. This number helps you understand your personal energy and direction.

5. Creating a Numeroscope

A Numeroscope, akin to an astrological chart, is created using the Lo-Shu Grid. By placing your Moolanka, Bhagyanka, and Kua Numbers along with other numbers in the grid, you can visualize your personal numerological map. This tool helps identify strengths, weaknesses, and potential life paths.

Chapter:4

1. The Concept of Yogas

In numerology, "Yogas" refers to specific patterns formed by numbers in the Lo-Shu Grid. These patterns indicate strengths and weaknesses in a person's numeroscope (birth chart) and can provide insights into their personality and life path.

2. The Lo-Shu Grid

The Lo-Shu Grid consists of 9 blocks, each representing a number and associated planet. By analyzing the presence and arrangement of numbers in this grid, we can understand different aspects of an individual's character and destiny.

3. The Horizontal Lines

The grid has three horizontal lines, each linked to different traits:

- The Mental Plane (4-9-2) indicates mental strength and intelligence.
- The Emotional or Soul Plane (3-5-7) reflects emotional sensitivity and a caring nature.
- The Practical Plane (8-1-6) shows a practical and logical approach to life.

4. The Vertical Lines

There are also three vertical lines:

- The Thought Plane (4-3-8) suggests strong analytical thinking and foresight.
- The Will Plane (9-5-1) represents strong willpower and resilience.
- The Action Plane (2-7-6) signifies action-oriented and industrious individuals.

5. The Diagonal Lines

Two diagonal lines, the *Super Success Line* (4-5-6) and the *Success Line* (2-5-8), indicate potential for great success. These lines, especially when complete, suggest that individuals are likely to achieve significant accomplishments and prosperity in life.

Chapter:5

1. Compatibility of Numbers and Planets

The unique concept is the compatibility of numbers from 1 to 9, each representing a planet. It draws parallels between planetary relationships in astrology and the interactions of these numbers in numerology, suggesting that certain numbers have inherent friendships, enmities, or neutrality toward each other.

2. Characteristics of Numbers

Each number has unique characteristics based on the planet it represents. For instance, 1 represents the Sun, seen as a kingly figure, while 2 represents the Moon, seen as a queen. Understanding these traits helps explain why certain numbers are compatible or incompatible.

3. Importance of Compatibility

The compatibility of numbers is significant in various aspects of life, such as relationships, business partnerships, and personal development. Compatibility can influence harmony and success, while incompatibility may lead to conflicts and challenges.

4. Neutral and Dual Relationships

Some numbers maintain neutral relationships or have dual relationships, being friendly under certain conditions and hostile under others. For example, the relationship between 4 (Rahu) and 8 (Saturn) can be friendly temporarily but may not survive in long-term partnerships.

5. Cultural and Mythological References

It is interesting to see integrated cultural and mythological stories, such as the tale of Rahu and Ketu from Hindu mythology, to illustrate the characteristics and relationships of the numbers. These stories provide a deeper understanding of the numbers' symbolic meanings and influence.

Chapter: 6

1. Individuality of Lucky and Unlucky Numbers:

The concept of lucky and unlucky numbers is subjective and varies from person to person. A number considered lucky for one individual may not be lucky for another. This is determined by the unique combination of their moolanka and bhagyanka.

2. Calculation of Lucky and Unlucky Numbers:

To identify lucky and unlucky numbers, both the moolanka and bhagyanka must be calculated from a person's date of birth. For example, for someone born on 19th June 1968, the moolanka is 1, and the bhagyanka is 4. The compatibility of numbers is then checked against a pre-defined chart to find common friends, neutral, and unfriendly numbers.

3. Importance of Compatibility Chart:

A compatibility chart helps in identifying which numbers are friends, neutral, or unfriendly to the moolanka and bhagyanka. This chart serves as a crucial tool for determining an individual's lucky and unlucky numbers, guiding them to make better choices based on these numbers.

4. Practical Application of Lucky Numbers:

Once identified, lucky numbers can be utilized in various aspects of life, such as selecting a vehicle number plate, house number, mobile number, or bank account number. This application is based on the belief that using lucky numbers can enhance positive outcomes in different areas of life.

5. Self-Verification and Practice:

To build confidence and verify the accuracy of the lucky and unlucky numbers, individuals are encouraged to calculate and analyze the numbers for themselves and their friends, family, and relatives. This practice not only strengthens their understanding of the concepts but also helps in making informed decisions based on numerological insights.

Chapter: 7

1. Unique Traits of Each Number

Each number from 1 to 9 in numerology is associated with specific characteristics influenced by the corresponding planet. These traits are reflected in individuals whose birth date is reduced to a particular number, referred to as the "Moolanka."

2. Categorization of Numbers

Each number can be further divided into categories based on the combined digits of the birth date. For example, number 1 is associated with 1, 10, 19, and 28, and these numbers are categorized as A, B, and C based on their qualities and planetary influences.

3. Personality Insights

You can find personality traits and potential life paths for individuals associated with each number. For example, those with the Moolanka number 1 are described as natural leaders, authoritative, and resilient, while those with the Moolanka number 2 are soft-hearted, diplomatic, and prone to mood swings.

4. Compatibility and Challenges

Certain numbers have been highlighted for their compatibility or potential challenges. For example, individuals with the number 28 (from Moolanka 1) may face struggles due to conflicting planetary influences, such as the moon (2) and Saturn (8).

5. Famous Personalities

The time examples of well-known individuals with each Moolanka number, illustrate how these characteristics manifest in real-life personalities.

Chapter :8

1. Vibrational Relationships

Moolanka (Life Path Number) and Bhagyanka (Destiny Number), combinations, can influence various aspects of life, including career, relationships, and overall success.

2. Role of Planetary Influences

The numbers are associated with specific planets, such as the Sun, Moon, Jupiter, and Saturn, which bring distinct characteristics and energies. These planetary influences shape the nature of each number combination.

3. Guidance for Career and Personal Life

It is the beauty of numerology that offers specific career and personal life guidance based on different number combinations, suggesting professions and areas of focus that align with the strengths and challenges of each combination.

4. Importance of Remedial Measures

For less favorable combinations, there is the possibility of remedial measures to mitigate challenges and enhance positive outcomes. The importance of understanding and addressing these influences is emphasized for achieving a balanced and successful life.

Chapter: 9

1. Definition and Calculation of Kua Number

The Kua number, also known as Ming Gua, is a personal number derived from one's date of birth and gender. The calculation method differs for males and females, reflecting the Yin and Yang energies associated with each gender. This number plays a role in Feng Shui and numerology, impacting one's life chart.

2. Role of Kua Number in Feng Shui

The Kua number, rooted in the Eight Aspirations Theory of Feng Shui, influences various aspects of an individual's life. It helps in balancing and strengthening one's birth chart by adding missing numbers, as illustrated with examples where the Kua number fills gaps in the Lo-Shu grid.

3. Impact and Significance

While the Kua number holds a lower weightage compared to Moolanka and Bhagyanka (25% versus 75% and 50%, respectively), it can still significantly influence one's numerological profile

Chapter: 10

1. Master Destiny Numbers

In numerology, master destiny numbers include 11, 22, and 33. These numbers are treated differently from regular numbers due to their unique and profound significance.

2. Characteristics of Master Destiny Numbers

11: People with this number tend to be big dreamers with high aspirations but may lack follow-through. They often need external support to realize their goals.

22: Known as "Master Builder," individuals with this number are both dreamers and doers. They set realistic goals, create plans, and are disciplined and resilient.

33: This number is associated with unconditional love, humanitarian work, and spiritual leadership.

3. Application in Predictions

When master destiny numbers are present, predictions should be based on these numbers (11, 22, 33) rather than their reduced single-digit forms (2, 4, 6).

Chapter:11

1. Concept of Karmic Debt Numbers

Karmic debt numbers (13, 14, 16, and 19) are believed to reflect unresolved issues from past lives. These numbers indicate areas where individuals may face challenges or lessons in their current life, connected to past mistakes or imbalances.

2. Specific Meanings of Karmic Numbers

13: Neglect of duties and the need for hard work and discipline.

14: Abuse of freedom, suggesting a need for healthy independence without rebellion.

16: Abuse of love, requiring a balance between materialism and spirituality.

19: Abuse of power, emphasizing the development of compassion and humanitarianism.

3. Opportunity for Growth

Karmic debt numbers are viewed not as burdens but as opportunities for personal growth and development. Understanding and addressing the challenges associated with these numbers can lead to a more balanced and fulfilling life.

"The Complete Book of Numerology... is a valuable means whereby our intuition and extrasensory perception (ESP) can develop and, in turn, improve all-around psychic awareness." - David A. Phillips

Chapter. 1

NUMEROLOGY-AN INTRODUCTION

"Numerology is the science of numbers, and each number has its own vibration and significance."- Juno Jordan

Welcome to this introductory chapter on numerology. I will talk about the basic concepts of numerology and the game of numbers. How different numbers combined with other numbers create Yogas in your Numeroscope. How can you calculate and prepare your numeroscope and know your future?

You may be excited to know the answers to many questions asked in your mind. Am I right? You purchased my book, which indicates that you are interested in numerology and ready to transform your life. Let us see the questions echoed in your mind.

- Does numerology really work for the upliftment of the birth chart?

- Is numerology a science or a myth?

- Is numerology a superstition in the eyes of modern science?

- Do we need to believe in numerology for our benefit?

- Is numerological prediction perfect?

- Can numerology do wonders in your life?

- Has it become a game-changer in others' lives?

- Is it a companion of failures or successful people?

So many questions may arise in your mind. If you believe in numerology people may raise an eyebrow and say something at your behind. If you don't believe many may **say "Oh my dear what happened? You don't believe in numerology, the number game?"** You have to understand what is right or wrong for you. you are your best judge. You may not live in peace if you lend an ear to anybody else. Let us explore the ethics of numbers.

ROLE OF NUMBERS IN YOUR LIFE

Numbers are present everywhere. Hans Decoz says;

"Numbers are the language of the universe, and through numerology, we can understand the deeper meanings of our lives."

Can you deny the presence of numbers in your life? Definitely not. Because from your birth to your death, even for every incarnation, numbers are with you. it will remain with you for an indefinite period. You can't deny it. Numbers and you appear to be inseparable. When numbers are the language of the universe and you are the product of the universe, then let the numbers unlock your **DESTINY.**

- ➤ When you are born there are numbers like date and time.

- ➤ When you start your education there is a number like the date of admission and roll number.

- ➤ When your result is declared you get the mark sheet consisting of numbers and percentages.

- ➤ When you get a job, you get a salary, and employee ID again consists of numbers.

- ➤ When you get married on a particular day it is a number.

- ➤ When you open a bank account you get an account number on a particular date.

- ➤ When you ask for a mobile number, you get a ten-digit number (it may vary in different countries).

- ➤ When you buy a motorcycle/car, you get the registration number on the number plate.

- ➤ When you travel on a bus, train, or flight you buy a ticket with a particular number.

- ➤ When you purchase some articles, you pay some currency in numbers.

- ➤ When you live in a house it bears a plot/house number.

- ➤ Your office, factory, farmhouse everything bears a number.

- ➤ When you are destined to die and leave this physical body it will also be attached with a number.

Now what did you learn from the above exercise? Number is everywhere, and you may not get rid of it. But learn to use the number for your best benefit.

In numerology, nine numbers starting from 1 to 9 are used to calculate the destiny of an individual. Zero is never used in numerology, unlike mathematics.

1 is the number that represents the **SUN**.

2 is the number that represents the **MOON**.

3 is the number that represents **JUPITER**.

4 is the number that represents **RAHU**

5 is the number that represents **MERCURY**.

6 is the number that represents **VENUS**.

7 is the number that represents **KETU**.

8 is the number that represents **SATURN**.

9 is the number that represents **MARS**.

In astrology, you can find all of the above planets and their effects on the horoscope. But in numerology, we use numbers to predict the future. Some planets are friends to each other and some are treated each other as enemies. Some planets behave neutrally. In our society, some behave friendly some act like enemies and few don't care about our cause, the same principles apply in numerology.

WHY YOUR DATE OF BIRTH IS SO SPECIAL?

Have you ever thought that you are unique and the secret is hiding in your date of birth? If you have not treated yourself special to date, you have done injustice to yourself. From now start loving yourself. You might have faced obstacles and setbacks in your life. Might have been disappointed with your fortune. You might have visited the astrologers but in vain. Believe me, the secret of your success is hiding in your date of birth. No date of birth is good or bad. God has given enough to you, but you could not find the diamond from it. Don't worry I will tell you the secret of your date of birth. Find out the best from it for your transformation. It will definitely reduce your struggle. Give a big smile on your face and increase your happiness and well-being. If you get your desired result you might say, yes numerology works. If the numerology could not find any solutions to your problem, you may say it doesn't work.

People always ask me one question, does numerology really work? The same question I have also asked my mentor. I am now sure that numerology works if applied intelligently. Let you try the concept of numerology in your life and see what happens. Knowledge is everywhere in the books, in our teachers, and on the internet. But unless you know the way to utilize it for excellence, the same knowledge is useless for you.

Let me tell you some of the secrets of your date of birth. In every date of birth, there are 81 combinations of MOOLANKA and BHAGYANKA. They indicate your life path and direction. You will be familiar with both the terms in the next chapters.

When we prepare a Numeroscope or birth chart from your date of birth, you cannot find the presence of all the 9 numbers, unlike a horoscope. You can find some numbers are present and some are missing from the date of birth. It is said out of one million one birth chat can witness the presence of all 9 numbers in the chart. It is definitely the rarest of rare events. You can find eight types of lines and eight types of Yogas in the Lo-Shu Grid. From the grid, we find the strengths and weaknesses of the individual. Now you can ask how you can find the hidden treasure from the chart. How can you overcome the weakness of your birth chart? Yes, you can get the answers to your questions later on. But I can assure you will be unstoppable if you come to know how to explore your strengths and overcome your weaknesses.

Numerology can explain everything you want to know.

You can find the missing numbers from your date of birth. The missing numbers indicate you are missing something in your life. But nothing to worry about. Every problem has a solution.

"Every problem has a solution; it may sometimes just need another perspective." -Katherine Russell

Numerology has the solution to the missing numbers.

Can you imagine your name spelling may foil your plan if not done according to your birth chart? Have you ever heard before that mere name spelling can change your fortune? Yes, different case studies suggest that 30-40% of your success or failure depends on your name spelling. If correct your name spelling according to your birth date you may get 30-40% more success in your life. I myself have corrected my name spelling and getting the benefit.

Further, we can predict your future years, months, and dates. Future predictions can help you to make better decisions for better predictions in your life. When you learn the secrets of success using numerology you can say YES in confidence that the "NUMEROLOGY WORKS 100%". If you want to learn numerology, keen interest is required for its perfection.

WHAT IS THERE FOR YOU IN THIS BOOK?

This book discusses the fundamentals of numerology. How to calculate Moolanka, bhagyanka, and Kua number. How to prepare the numeroscope from any date of birth. The beauty of numerology is it only needs a date of birth, no day, time, or place of birth is required, unlike astrology. Do you believe one can choose it as a profession? The answer is Yes if you complete all the courses sincerely and train properly. If you give proper attention and do hard as well as smart work you can earn lakhs of rupees per month. If you are in a good profession and happy then no issue, you may use it as your passive income.

You can implement the science of numerology in your life for your perfection. Remember no one is perfect on this planet. Everyone has the scope to improve. Capacity building and acquiring knowledge give anyone more power. You can use it for the improvement of your family members like your parents, wife/husband, children, friends, and relatives. Imagine you're a small piece of advice that may do wonders in anyone's life. Can put a smile on the lips of many. Then why not implement it? Remember, learning is a continuous process and empowers you more.

Chapter .2

ORIGIN, TYPES OF NUMEROLOGY AND LO-SHU GRID

"Numbers are the universal language offered by nature to humanity." - Galileo Galilei (Italian astronomer and physicist)

Numerology is a science of numbers. It can create magic in your life with its proper applications. As I discussed earlier our lives are based on the magic of numbers whether we understand it or not. Numbers are there everywhere. They are part of our journey and ultimate destiny. We are born with numbers and will die with numbers. Without our awareness numbers act like time. Let us discuss a date of birth such as 12th February 1968. Here we find 1, 1, 2, 2, 6,8, 9. In this particular case 1 and 2 are repeated twice and 6,8 and 9 find their place once. Other numbers like 3, 4, 5, 6, 7 are missing. But when we further proceed to prepare the numeroscope with the help of the Lo-Shu grid we can find the Moolanka, bhagyanka, and Kua number, where we may find more numbers to complete the birth chat. However, the chart preparation may be a little bit different in different types of numerology.

When you will know the magic of numbers, you will be amazed and mesmerized. All the secrets are there in your birth chart. Your success, career, partner, money, children, happiness, love, respect, health, failure everything. Do you want to make yourself happy, healthy, wealthy, and respected, or languish in poverty, failure, and suffering? I know you are intelligent enough to prefer your perfection and opt for happiness.

ORIGIN OF NUMEROLOGY?

The exact origin of numerology is shrouded in the mists of time, but there's evidence of its use in various cultures across history.

Ancient Civilizations (3000 BC and onwards): Traces of numerology appear in Mesopotamia (Babylon and Assyria), Egypt, China, and Greece. These cultures believed numbers held hidden meanings and used them for divination (predicting the future) and understanding the universe.

Mesopotamia: Numbers were associated with celestial bodies and used in astrology.

Egypt: Numbers were seen as having a divine essence and were used in constructing sacred structures and rituals.

China: The I Ching, an ancient Chinese divination text, uses numerical relationships to interpret the world.

Pythagoras (6th century BC): Often considered the **"father of numerology"** in the West. He believed numbers were the key to understanding the universe and assigned meanings to them. His ideas influenced Western numerology for centuries.

Middle Ages: Numerology faced challenges during this period. The rise of Christianity viewed some numerological practices as heretical. However, numerology continued to be practiced in some areas, and some alchemical theories were linked to it.

Renaissance (15th-17th centuries): Renewed interest in numerology emerged. Philosophers like Giordano Bruno explored numerological ideas, and mystics used them for divination.

19th and 20th centuries: Numerology gained popularity in the West, particularly in the early 20th century. It continues to be practiced by some today, with various schools of thought and interpretations.

Vedic Numerology:

<u>Roots in Vedic Tradition</u>: Vedic Numerology stems from the Vedas, the ancient scriptures of Hinduism. It integrates numerological concepts with Vedic astrology and the philosophy of Samkhya.

<u>Emphasis on Planets and Karma:</u> Unlike some numerology systems that focus on core numbers 1-9. Vedic Numerology incorporates the nine planets (including Rahu and Ketu) from Vedic astrology. These planets are believed to influence your life path and karma.

<u>Core Numbers and Destiny:</u> Vedic Numerology uses calculations based on your birthdate to derive core numbers like your PSYCHIC NUMBER (derived from the day of birth) and DESTINY NUMBER (derived from your entire birthdate). These numbers offer insights into your personality, strengths, and potential life path.

<u>Unique Features:</u> Here are some aspects that distinguish Vedic Numerology from other systems:

Inclusion of Rahu and Ketu, the shadow planets in Vedic astrology.

Focus on karmic influences and past life connections.

Use mantras and gemstones associated with your numbers.

While numerology's origins are ancient, its specific practices and interpretations have evolved throughout history. Remember, numerology is not considered a scientific discipline, but it offers a fascinating perspective on the relationship between numbers and human experience.

TYPES OF NUMEROLOGY

We can find mainly 6 types of numerology practiced worldwide. Such as;

- Chinese numerology

- Vedic numerology

- Cheiro numerology

- Chaldean numerology

- Pythagorean numerology

41

- Western numerology

Out of the above, we shall synthesize the important elements and prepare a simple technique for better understanding and practice. However, our basic concept will be Chinese numerology, which talks about the Loshu Grid. We will also use Vedic and Cheiro numerology. Cheiro is called the hero of numerology. Many respect him as the God of numerology. We use his technique for name spelling correction.

The Lo-Shu grid concept comes from Chinese numerology. Now I feel you are excited to know why the term is called Lo-Shu grid.

The Lo Shu Grid gets its name from the Luo River (Lo-Shu in pinyin) near Luoyang, Henan in China. Legend says a giant turtle (sometimes referred to as a "divine turtle") emerged from the Yellow River carrying the Lo Shu grid pattern on its back.

According to legend, the Lo Shu Square, a 3x3 magic square where the numbers 1 to 9 are arranged such that the sum of the numbers in each row, column, and diagonal equals 15, was revealed to Saint Lo-Shu by a turtle. This event was seen as a sign of good fortune, and the pattern was named after Saint Lo-Shu, who had seen the grid first on the back of the tortoise.

LO-SHUGRID

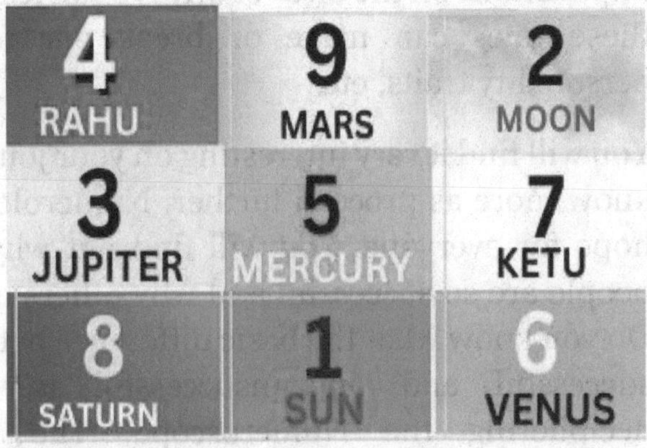

The above image is called the Lo-Shu Grid. It is also called LAXMI YANTRA in India.

It has 9 blocks in 3x3 format. Each block is represented with one number from 1-9. You can see that the grid has 3 vertical, 3 horizontal, and two diagonal lines. All the lines form separate **Yoga** in numerology. But the grid is formed so intelligently and scientifically that if you count the numbers in any line, you will find a sum total of 15. Isn't it amazing? All the credit goes to Lo-Shu, the creator of the grid. Further, if you add 1 and 5(15), you will get 6. Number 6 represents

Venus, the planet of luxury, success, and glamor. Each line bears a specific name and represents the specific characteristics. We will learn each and every aspect of the line, their importance and implications on the birth chart. We can learn how these lines can make or break our fortune, personality traits, etc.

You will find it very interesting on your journey to know more as proceed further. Numerology is a hope for everyone. You will find out why some people are so successful and why others are not. Do you know what the basic difference between a successful and an unsuccessful is? It is deciphering the Numeroscope. The proper analysis of the birth chart can make you unstoppable and overcome weakness.

Be optimistic and happy. Many more things will follow for your empowerment in the next chapters.

Chapter.3

LOTTERIES AND NUMEROSCOPE

"In numerology, your life path number is considered the most significant number in your personal numerology chart. It reveals your most fulfilling life direction and the major lessons you are here to learn during this lifetime." – Anonymous

I feel you are now more interested to know more about numerology. In this chapter, I will introduce you to three lotteries and how to prepare a numeroscope by yourself without the help of an expert.

What are Lotteries in Numerology?

You might have heard of lotteries. You might have played lotteries at a fair once or more to get a chocolate, a hat, or a candy in your childhood. In the lottery, the ringmaster or the shopkeeper must have given you a few rings to encircle an object. Or you have been given a toy gun to strike a balloon. If you strike the object, you get the destined prize or it is said your lottery is full. If you become unsuccessful it is presumed that your lottery is empty.

Sometimes at a young age, you might have tried once or more to try your luck by purchasing a lottery ticket to promote an event. After the lottery is drawn, you try to match the number of your lottery ticket with the number announced as the winner. If you win your lottery is said to be full otherwise it is empty. The same logic is also applied in numerology in a different way.

From the date of birth, we can find out whether your lottery is filled in or left empty. Every date of birth can have three lotteries. Are you excited to know about the lotteries in your date of birth? What are they and their effects on your life? How can you use them in your favor?

Let me explain how to calculate a lottery from a date of birth. Each date of birth can have three lotteries.

For example, 13.08. 1967 is the date of birth of X.

The first lottery is the Moolanka. Moolanka of X is the date only. In this instance case it is 13. As said in numerology, we have to add a double-digit number to a single digit. Now when we add (1+3) we can get 4. Now the Moolanka of X comes to **4.**

Now proceed to the second lottery number the **bhagyanka.** Now how can we calculate the bhagyanka? It is very simple. It is the total sum of

X's birth date, month, and year. In this case, the date is 13, the month is 8, and the year is 1967. The sum total of all the digits comes to (1+3+8+1+9+6+7)35 and the sum of 35 comes to (3+5) 7. Now we get the bhagyanka of X as 7.

You may ask one question if the sum total of a date of birth comes to 10 or 20, what can be considered as the correct number? I have told you earlier that in numerology 0 is not considered as a number. Hence in the case of 10, it can be said one, and in place of 20, you can count it as 2.

Another important terminology often used is **PSYCHIC NUMBER** in numerology for MOOLANKA. Similarly, the bhagyanka is often called by the name **DESTINY NUMBER** or **LIFE PATH NUMBER.**

Now the next and third lottery number left is called **(PA)KUA NUMBER.** Calculation of this number from a date of birth is a little bit interesting. Because its calculation is different in the case of males and females. Here only birth year is needed for calculation. Let us calculate. Take the birth year of X. It is 1967. The addition of the total numbers 1+9+6+7 comes to 23 or 2+3 =5. Consider X as a male and his Kua number can be calculated as **11-5=6.**

Now **KUA NUMBER OF X** comes to 6. But you may ask why the sum total of the birth year is subtracted from 11. The answer is it is a formula.

Follow the principle "PUT THE FORMULA AND GET THE ANSWER."

Now it is the turn of a female. Let a **female Y** born in the year 1967. We can calculate the Kua number of Y by adding 4 to the sum total of birth year. Her birth year total is (1+9+6+7=23=2+3) is 5. Now **KUA NUMBER OF Y** shall be **5+4=9.**

Now I am confident that you are comfortable in calculating the Kua number in the case of male and female. In the instance case, Kua number of X(male) comes to **6,** and Kua number of Y(Female) comes to **9.**

Now we got all the three lottery numbers from above. Now are you excited to know whether the lottery of X and Y are filled or empty?

The date of birth of X is 13.08. 1967.

- **Moolanka is 4**

- **Bhagyanka is 7**

- **Kua number is 6 in the case of males and 9 in the case of females.**

Can you see moolanka number 4 on the above date of birth? You can say no, it is not found. Hence it is considered that the **lottery of X is filled concerning his Moolanka**. If the moolanka number is seen in a date of birth, it is said that the lottery is empty.

Now move further and see whether the lottery of the bhagyanka is filled or left empty. Now bhagyanka 7 is present in the date of birth (year of birth). Hence second lottery concerning the date of birth is empty.

In some circumstances, you can find both the bhagyanka and moolanka are the same. If they are found missing from their date of birth, then it will be considered that one lottery is filled and another is empty. It can't be considered that both the lotteries are filled or empty.

Let us see the lottery of the Kua number. Now I see 6 is the Kua no of X(male) and it is present in his date of birth. Hence, his third lottery is empty. Then whether the lottery of Y(Female) filled or left empty? Can you guess now? You are right third lottery of Y is empty, as 9 is present in the date of birth.

You are now a little bit confused regarding the empty or full lottery. I was also confused but after thorough study, I came to know the truth. I have told you earlier that the Lo-Shu grid contains 9 blocks. Every block represents a number. When we talk about a lottery it means one unfilled block is getting a number. The lottery is empty means the same number is already present in the block earlier. The lottery in respect of more numbers is filled up means more blocks are filled in the Numeroscope.

Hope you now understand everything I have discussed till now. Thanks for your interest in this topic. Let us move further to understand how to prepare a Numeroscope.

Now again consider the **date of birth of X is 13.08. 1967.**

NUMEROSCOPE

<table>
<tr><td>4
RAHU</td><td>9
MARS</td><td>2
MOON</td></tr>
<tr><td>3
JUPITER</td><td>5
MERCURY</td><td>7
KETU</td></tr>
<tr><td>8
SATURN</td><td>1
SUN</td><td>6
VENUS</td></tr>
</table>

LO-SHU GRID

"Numerology, like astrology, predicts future trends and patterns by analyzing the numbers in your life." — Anonymous

An astrologer prepares a horoscope from a date, place, and time of birth. Numerologists prepare a Numeroscope from date of birth only. For the preparation of a birth chart or Numeroscope, the

50

Lo-Shu grid is considered a guiding compass. Now look at the Lo-Shu Grid and the position of the number in the grid. See carefully the 9 blocks and the position of the numbers. Take a piece of paper and prepare a grid on it. Fill the numbers in the grid as per the Lo-Shu grid. Place all numbers 1, 3, 8, 1, 9, 6, 7 at the proper place. Now place the Moolanka, bhagyanka, and Kua number accordingly.

However, remember one thing. If your moolanka is coming from one single digit (such as 1 to 9) you need not fill it again. In the above instance, case 4 is the moolanka and needs to be filled in.

Have you prepared the Numeroscope of X? If not prepare it now. I am giving you 5 minutes for the purpose. Ok fine. You have done it. Now see the numeroscope I have prepared. Tally it now with yours.

4	9	
3		77
8	11	66

D-4, C-7, K-6

Now take the examples of two more males named AKASH and PARESH.

Consider the date of birth of Akash is 15.02.1987.

4	9	2
	5	7
8	11	66

Akash: D-6, C-6, K-4

in this case, moolanka and bhagyanka are the same as 6 and the Kua number is 4. As 1 and 6 are repeating they find their place twice in the grid.

Now consider the date of birth of Paresh as **06.01.1987.**

4	9	
	5	7
8	11	6

What do you observe in this chart? 6 is not repeated as a moolanka, because 6 is a single digit and is already present in the chart.

Let me explain and prepare the Numeroscope of two women. Consider their name as LISA and SARA.

The date of birth of LISA is 10.03.1987

	9	22
3		7
8	11	

LISA: D-1, C-2, K-2

In this birth chart, the moolanka is 1, the bhagyanka is 2, and Kua's number is also 2. As the moolanka is 1 and her date of birth is 10 or say 1, the same number can't be entered again. Further, both the bhagyanka and Kua number are the same as 2, and it is not found in the date of birth, 2 is placed twice in the chart.

Now let's talk about the birth chart of SARA. Her date of birth **is 19.03.1987.** Her moolanka, bhagyanka, and Kua numbers are the same as LISA's. Now prepare the birth chart.

<table>
<tr><td></td><td>99</td><td>22</td></tr>
<tr><td>3</td><td></td><td>7</td></tr>
<tr><td>8</td><td>111</td><td></td></tr>
</table>

SARA-D-1, C-2, K-2

Now you see the difference between the two birth charts. In the chart of LISA 1 is coming two times and it is coming three times in respect of SARA. Similarly, 9 is coming once in the case of **LISA** and two times in **SARA**'s chart.

I feel you are now very happy and confident to prepare a Numeroscope without any confusion. Now prepare your Numeroscope along with your family members. It will definitely give you confidence to proceed further. Let me talk about the dimensions of both charts. In the charts not a single line is complete, which indicates that both the numeroscopes are weak and three blocks are blanks. In the subsequent chapters, I will talk about the 81 combinations of moolanka and bhagyanka and their implications on the person.

Chapter.4

8 YOGAS IN NUMEROLOGY

"Everything around us is made up of numbers. To understand nature, we must think in numbers." – Pythagoras

You might have heard about different Yogas in Numerology. If not heard no problem. We all are in the learning process on the right path to acquiring knowledge. Yoga talks about the strengths and weaknesses of the Numeroscope. Unless you analyze it, you can't judge the birth chart. Now can you remember the position of numbers in the Lo-Shu Grid? If yes fine. If can't remember nothing to worry about. Its 9 blocks represent different numbers and planets. I am presenting the same before you again.

4 **RAHU**	9 **MARS**	2 **MOON**
3 **JUPITER**	5 **MERCURY**	7 **KETU**
8 **SATURN**	1 **SUN**	6 **VENUS**

LO-SHU GRID

Now again you see the Lo-Shu Grid above and 8 lines consisting of 3 numbers each. As I have told you earlier there are 3 horizontal, 3 vertical, and 2 diagonal lines seen in the Lo-Shu grid.

HORIZONTAL LINES OR PLANES

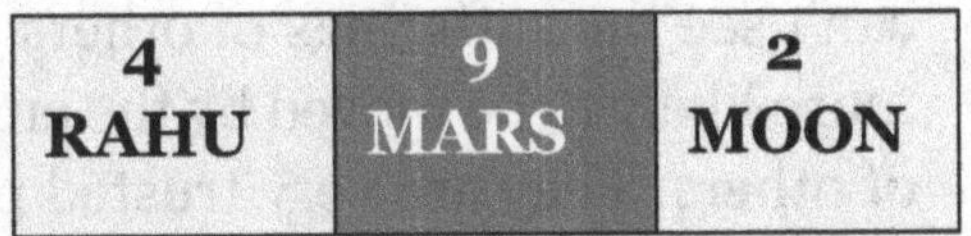

4 **RAHU**	9 **MARS**	2 **MOON**

Now we see 4, 9, and 2 constitute the first horizontal line, where 4 represents Rahu, 9 represents Mars and 2 represents the Moon. This line is called **MENTAL PLANE**. Then what does it indicate? If all three numbers are present in a numeroscope, indicates that the person is brilliant a god-gifted brain. Can remember things easily without much effort. He is mentally very strong and can do something unique. The people born in the last century have a common 9 whereas 2 is common for the people born in this current century. What do you learn from the first horizontal line? What is the message for us? The message is planets like Rahu, Mars, and Moon create a Yoga in the birth chart making the person brilliant and sharp-minded.

3	5	7
JUPITER	**MERCURY**	**KETU**

Now see the second horizontal line formed taking 3,5 and 7 numbers. This particular line is called **EMOTIONAL OR SOUL PLANE.** The people having such lines are very emotional and sentimental. They are very soft-hearted. They can't see the sufferings of others. They are much more likely to be moved by the emotional appeals of others. They are very trusted people and trust others easily. For this type of tendency, they are often cheated by others in their lives. They easily be fooled by others.

The tagline for these types of people is "they are people of golden heart. The heart rules not the head. You can trust them blindly without a second thought."

8 SATURN	1 SUN	6 VENUS

The third horizontal line is formed containing 8, 1, and 6. This line is called **PRACTICAL PLANE.** People having this line in their numeroscope are very practical in their approach to actions and logical-minded. Before taking up a project they go deep into the 5 W. W means what, why, when, where, and wow?

- What types of projects?

- Why to execute?

- When to execute with the timeline?

- Where to execute with its feasibilities? And

- When understand everything says "Wow."

They possess an analytical brain. They don't believe anyone easily. You can't convince them easily or win their hearts. They are not to be emotionally exploited. You may not win them logically. They try to apply logic to everything for which they are misunderstood sometimes.

VERTICAL PLANES

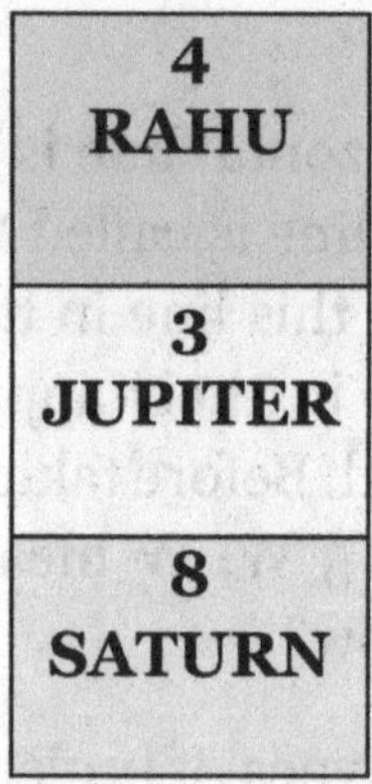

Let me talk about the vertical plane. The first vertical line contains 4,3 and 8 numbers. This line is called **THOUGHT PLANE**. If a numeroscope has this vertical line complete, it is presumed that the person is a thinker. His thought process is very strong. He is a very farsighted man. He can judge the market sentiment in advance. He can anticipate profit or loss in business in the future. His actions are based on well-articulated thought and reasoning. They can take a calculated risk. For example, he can buy a property for 10 lakhs for now eyeing for 1 crore after ten years, which can't be anticipated by a common man. After 10 years he can get the amount more or less than one crore. In fact, they are disciplined, well organized, well planned, and can visualize things better.

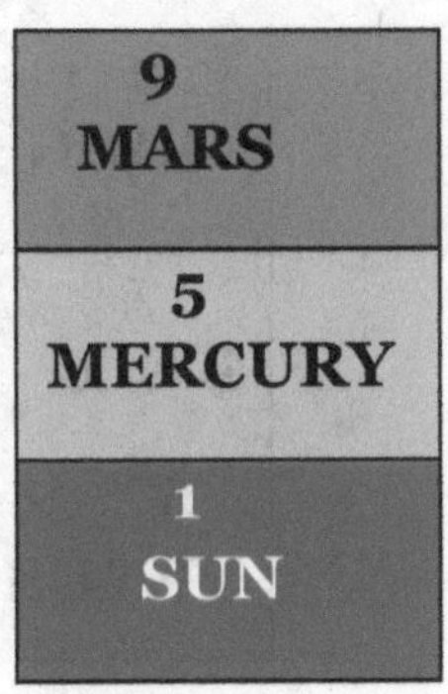

The second vertical line contains 9, 5, and 1 numbers. This plane is called **WILL PLANE.** It indicates that people with a will plane, in their birth chart have very strong willpower. The people are resilient. In fact, you may say they are real fighters. They are capable of handling the hard situations and bounce back from setbacks. They never bow down to any adverse situations including financial, emotional, or physical situations. They appear very calm from the outside. You can't understand the people by merely seeing their faces. I can quote the word sthi-ta-pra-jña(स्थितप्रज्ञ) for them.

In this line 5 makes the difference. A line without 5 may not give such balance in life.

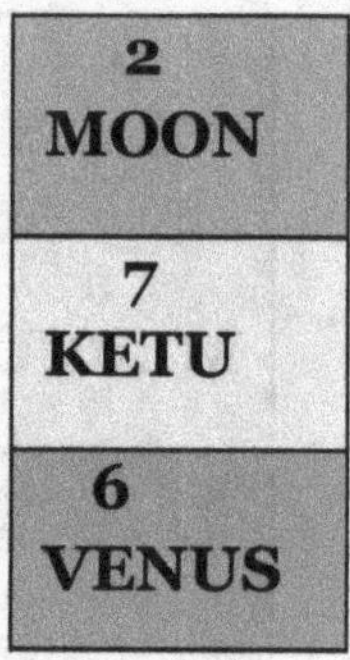

The nest vertical line can have 2,7 and 6. This line is called **ACTION PLANE.** People having this line in their numeroscope are action-takers and industrious. They can achieve their goals by taking timely actions. Once decided they chalk out a plan to execute it. Their lives are full of action, action, and action. For them "impossible is a word that is found in a fool's dictionary."

Now two diagonal lines are left to explain.

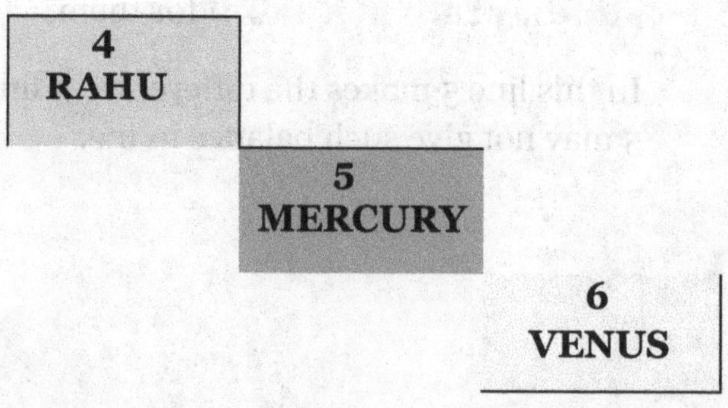

The first diagonal lines are 4,5, and 6, known as the **SUPER SUCCESS LINE.** These number forms a yoga known as **RAJ YOGA** or **GOLDEN YOGA.** In a horoscope, many Yogas are seen. People having this line in their numeroscope are super successful in their lives. They can have names, fame, happiness, and money. No doubt they are action-takers but success touches their feet. They never face major setbacks in their lives. They may or may not born rich but soon rise to name and fame with their luck and endeavors. You may call them lucky champs. Check your birth chart. You may have such a line of supper success.

Some examples of such types of people;

- ✓ Baba Ramdev-Yoga Guru and Entrepreneur

- ✓ Shri Shri Ravisankar- Spiritual leader with international repute.

- ✓ Amir Khan-Very successful and famous Film actor

- ✓ Sonia Gandhi- Widow of Rajiv Gandhi (former premier of India) and Political leader (chairman of UPA/INDI alliance)

✓ Sanjay Lila Bhansali- Famous film director.

✓ Anil Kapoor-Film actor and producer in India.

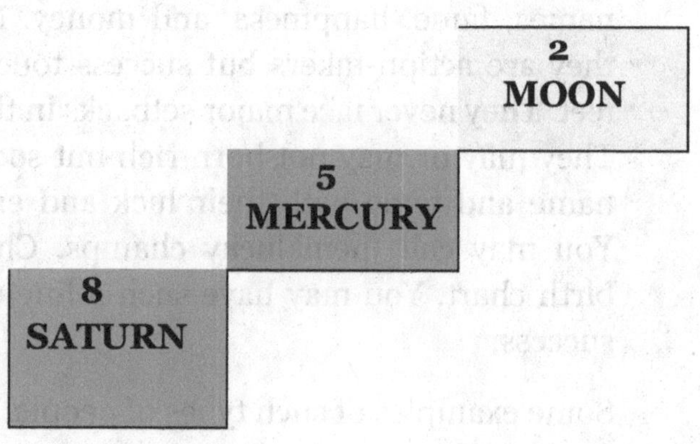

The second diagonal line contains the numbers 2,5 and 8. This line is **CALLED SUCCESS LINE** or **SILVER YOGA.** The people having success line in their numeroscope ought to be successful in their lives. As 2,5 and 8 are earth elements, businesses related to earth like real estate, agriculture, and the stock market can suit them better. They can make a lot of money from such types of business. They can have won a home early. The presence of 8 in this line makes them rich, live in rich and die in rich. You might have such silver yoga, check now.

64

Now all 8 lines and their importance have been explained. Hope you have understood it better and can able to utilize it for the improvement of your life as well as the lives of others.

Now you may ask in the numeroscope of many people we may find the missing numbers from the line. Then what would be the percentage of the success? Yes, you are right, you can find many people with weak birth charts, leaving them unsuccessful.

Let me take the Numeroscope of **Akash (15.02. 1987) and** Paresh **(06.01.1987).**

4	9	2
	5	7
8	11	66

Akash (15.02. 1987)

4	9	
	5	7
8	11	6

Paresh (06.01.1987).

You see both the numeroscopes and find the differences. What do you have observed? In the case of Akash, the first and third horizontal lines are complete. Similarly, the second and third horizontal lines are complete. Both the diagonal lines are also complete. In the case of Akash, only one block is vacant and other blocks are filled. It is a very strong chart and he can get all sorts of names, fame, money, long life, and happiness in life.

Now see the birth chart of Paresh. Here one vertical, one horizontal, and one diagonal line are complete. Only one missing number 2 makes huge differences between the two numeroscopes. This chart is very strong. In comparison to Akash, Paresh is likely to get less success in life. However, his life can be improved if remedial measures are being made.

Both the numeroscopes presented above are rare. You can't find one such a chart in thousands.

Remember that more missing numbers mean more weakness in numeroscope and a lesser degree of success rate.

Chapter.5

COMPATIBILITY OF NUMBERS

"Numbers have an important story to tell. They rely on you to give them a voice" – Stephen Few

Welcome to the amazing chapter on the compatibility of numbers. In the previous chapters, you become familiar with the numbers from 1 to 9. Every number represents a planet. In astrology, an astrologer predicts your future by observing the position of planets in your horoscope, but we predict your future from your numeroscope. In our society, you may have some good friends, some neutral people who meet during morning walks, and some enemies. Why are some friends, some enemies, and some neutral? Why all are not your friends or enemies? Can you find out any reason behind it? It is because of our qualities, characters, choices, thinking patterns, behavior, financial and social status, etc. But we can improve our relationships and neutralize the foes with our efforts.

This topic is significant for future endeavors and predictions of the future more correctly.

It is also required to match the compatibility of two persons, find out the lucky number, and lucky color, and most importantly for name spelling corrections.

Now let us get started. Again, for your convenience see the Lo-Shu grid to know the numbers with their associated planets.

4 RAHU	9 MARS	2 MOON
3 JUPITER	5 MERCURY	7 KETU
8 SATURN	1 SUN	6 VENUS

CHARACTERISTICS OF NUMBERS

Let us see the characteristics of the numbers from 1 to 9.

1. Number one is the Sun, the source of all energies in the solar system. Sun is king of all planets. Hence 1 is king of all numbers starting from 1 to 9.
2. Number 2 is the moon. Moon bears all the qualities of a queen. Moon is called the queen.

3. Number 3 is attributed to Jupiter. Jupiter is the teacher or guru of gods. He is called Devguru, a councilor of gods.

4. Number 4 represents Rahu. Rahu is good for the poor and bad for the rich. He plunders the wealth of the rich and distributes it among the poor. His character resembles a gangster. He is the god of the poor but the enemy of the rich. As he bears only a head without a heart or body, he only thinks from his head. You may not get mercy from number 4.

5. Number 5 is mercury. He is treated as the prince in numerology. A king, queen, and prince constitute a royal family.

6. Number 6 is Venus. Venus is guru of Danav. He is a councilor and advisor of Demons. This number symbolizes enjoyment, glamor, fashion, money, family, and conjugal relationships.

7. Number 7 represents Ketu. It is the lower part of Rahu known as the shadow planet.

Now let us enjoy the related myth of Rahu and Ketu. The mythological story goes like this. After the Samudra Manthan (churning of the ocean)jointly by both demons and gods, all the elements, and the precious items including *Kamadhenu* (The wish-fulfilling divine cow), *Uchhaishravas* (A magnificent white horse), *Airavata* (A celestial white elephant), *Kaustubha* (A precious gem), *Parijata* (A divine flowering tree), *Varuni* (The goddess of wine), *Apsaras* (Celestial nymphs), *Chandra* (The moon), *Dhanvantari* (The divine physician), *Lakshmi* (The goddess of wealth and prosperity), evolved from it taken away by gods and Rishis, leaving none for the demons, although both have contributed for the purpose. Lastly, *Amrit* came out of the ocean. Lord Vishnu in the guise of a beautiful woman distributed it to the gods. However, in the guise of God Rahu has eaten the nectar. When Vishnu realized the presence of Rahu, he chopped the head making two separate parts by his *Sudaran Chakra*(discus). As Rahu consumed the nectar did not die and both parts remained alive.

The character of Ketu is that he can't think from his head due to its absence. He does think from the heart. He speaks the language of the associated number. In the other language, if he is fitted with the head of the sun, he acts like a king. If he is fitted with the head of Rahu he gets its complete form. He can behave as per the head he is likely to get.

8. Number 8 is the number of Saturn, the god of justice. He judges himself. He gives awards, rewards, or punishment according to your karma(actions). Have you seen judges in the judiciary system?

They only pronounce the order on the basis of the available facts, documents, arguments, and written submissions produced before them. They have no friends or enemies. They are supposed to be neutral.

9. This number represents Mars. He is treated as a commander but pious.

Now you have a glimpse of the characteristics of the numbers. But we are not aware how they can behave if come together. It is a real game the compatibility of numbers.

COMPATIBILITY OF NUMBERS

Every number has some friends, non-friends, and neutral numbers. Let me draw a table for better appreciation.

No	Friends	Non-Friends	Neutral
1	9,2,5,3,6,1	8	4,7
2	1,5,3,2	8,4,9	6,7
3	1,5,3,2,7*	6	4,8,9,7*
4	7,1,5,6,4*,8*	4*,8*,2,9	3
5	1,2,3,6,5	....	7,8,9,4

6	1,5,7,6	3	8,9,2,4
7	4,6,1,3,5	....	2,8,9,7
8	5,6,3,7,4*,8*	(4*,8*,)1,2,	9
9	1,5,3	4,2	6,7,8,9

Let me explain the above chart in detail.

NUMBER **1**

1 represents the sun, the king of the planetary system. The sequence of friends is as follows 9,2,5,3,6,1. You can say it is the king's number. It is royal in his approach and attitude. He runs an empire. What does a king need to run a kingdom, an empire? Expand the empire? Annex and conquer the kingdom of the enemy? Can you guess? It is obviously an army or military power. Who is the commander of the military? The answer is no 9, Mars. That is why 1 king is very close to Commander 9. The king can share some secrets with the commander only. It can't even be shared with his beloved wife (queen). Our history witnesses the mutiny of the commanders against kings and the seizure of power by army commanders. Now it is clear that the king is nearest to 9.

After number 9, next nearer to number 1 is number 2, the queen. If you want peace in family and conjugal life, you must love, care, and respect your wife, otherwise, your life will be no less than hell. King is not an exception to it.

Then comes 5, the prince, 3, 6 the councilors, and 1(king) in decreasing orders of priority as shown in the table. You may ask how 1 is a friend of 1. One answer is self-love, and another answer is a king needs to keep good relations with his counterparts in the neighboring states for peace and prosperity in the region.

Now let's talk about the non-friend column. Here 8, Saturn is the lonely enemy of 1, the Sun. why Saturn is the enemy of the Sun?

There is a myth, Saturn is the illegitimate child of Sun, born to mother Chaya. Sun entered into a relationship with Chaya but did not get her married or recognize her as his wife. The son born to their relationship, Saturn was very dark in complex, for which the sun did not acknowledge him as his son. Saturn demands his recognition as the son of the sun, but the sun refuses it, rather than offering a palace, money, property, etc. As the matter was not settled amicably, Saturn maintained his enmity with his father the sun forever.

In a neutral column, you can find 4 and 7. One is gangster and another is headless. A king doesn't need their support at the same time and may not apply his forces against them.

NUMBER 2

Number 2 is queen. In the friends list you can see this 1,5,3,2 sequence. Who comes first as a friend of the queen? It is king, her beloved husband. Can a CHEST WIFE live without her husband? The answer is known to you. After the king, the queen needs her son, the prince of the empire, the future king. Then comes 3, the councilor. In the time of crisis, his advice can save the kingdom. Next comes 2, the queen and her counterparts.

Now see her non-friend's column. Who are they? 8,4,9. First comes 8, Saturn the stepson. A friendly relationship between a stepmother and a stepson may not normally exist. If we see it from a scientific point of view, the moon represents water, and Saturn represents iron. The combination of iron and water makes the iron rust. It is better for them to keep their distance. That is why both 2 and 8 can't stay together in a single column.

4 is gangster. Queen doesn't like gangsters, and as a woman, one should not like such an unworthy fellow. Next comes number 9, the commander. Queen hates the commander because the king spends most of his time consulting with 9. Further, 9 does not take command from the queen except the king.

Next, come the neutral planets of the moon. Numbers 6 and 7 are neutral to number 2. Because the queen rarely needs the advice of Venus. Jupiter is always available to guide the queen as and when necessary. Ketu (7) is headless, how can he support the queen? Number 2 has no enmity or friendship with Ketu. He is left as neutral.

NUMBER 3

Number 3 is Jupiter, the guru of gods. He is pious and vegetarian. His friends come in the following sequence; 1,5,3,2,7*. He is most friendly with the king. Next comes 5, the prince as his friend. The next friend of Jupiter is Jupiter himself. Here both are councilors and respect each other. Number 3 has no problem with 2 or queen. Jupiter is the symbol of knowledge. 7 is the symbol of wisdom. Knowledge and wisdom have a positive equation making them friends.

Number 6 is positioned as a non-friend of number 3. You may ask why. Both 3 and 6 are councilors, both are powerhouses of knowledge. Then why they are non-friends? Because there is a basic difference between the two. 3 is the councilor of gods/devata and 6 is the councilor of demons/danav (Asuras). Both are from different ideologies, as gods and demons are enemies to each other.

Further, 4,8,9,7 are neutral for Jupiter. Because number 3, has no business with 4,8,9,7 (7 may become his friend sometimes due to his wisdom).

NUMBER 4

Number 4 is Rahu. Can you tell me who would be his best friend? I think you guessed it correctly. It is number 7, Ketu, the lower part of Rahu. The combination of 4 and 7 not only completes the body but also completes the thinking pattern. 4 is a good gangster he needs the support of the king to remain in freedom. That is why made friends with 5, the future king. Next comes 6, in his friend list, because both share a common character.

2 and 9 are non-friends of 4. Because the queen doesn't need the support of a gangster or believe in him, the characteristics of 9 and 4 are completely different.

Now 4 & 8, both may be friends if their relationship is not permanent. Both may be non-friends if their relationships are made permanent. You are now a little bit confused by the above statement. Am I right? Let me explain if the people of 4 moolanka number make friends, then it is okay. But if the simple friendship turns into a permanent relationship in the form of marriage, or business partner it can't survive.

You find only Jupiter in the neutral column. Gangsters may seek the advice of Jupiter but number 3 keeps a safe distance from it.

NUMBER 5

Number 5 is Mercury, the prince. The sequence of friends comes as follows 1,2,3,6,5. The prince is closer to his father, the king, then his mother comes second. He has a good rapport with both the councillors 3 and 6. A prince has a good friendship with another prince. Hence 5 is a friend of 5.

It is important to note that a prince has no non-friend. Because when you see the Lo-Shu Grid you can find that 5 is positioned at the center, keeping an equal distance from all the blocks. As a prince 5, maintain neutrality with 7,8,9,4. Similarly, 7,8,9,4 have no problem with the future king 5.

NUMBER 6

Number 6 is Venus, the guru of demons. He believes in merrymaking and the goodness of demons. As a councilor, he is close to the king. Next in closeness come 5, the prince. Number 7, (Ketu) is also his friend because 7 is the disciple of 6. Further, number 6 is the friend of 6, a councilor can be a friend of a councilor.

6 has one non-friend in 3. Because 6 is the guru of demons and 3 is the guru of gods. Both can't see each other, as both are anti-planet. Next, come the neutral numbers in the form of 8,9,2,4. They have no problem with 6.

NUMBER 7

Number 7 is Ketu. I have told you earlier that Ketu is a shadow planet and the myth behind it. It has no head. Now can you guess who would be his best friend? I feel your presumption is right. It is Rahu, number 4. When 7 is associated with 4 a complete structure is formed, as if they are made for each other. The next close friend of Ketu is Venus, number 6. Venus is the mentor of 7. They have a relationship of teacher and disciple. Next comes number 1, the king. Being headless he thinks from heart for which he needs the blessings of the king. Jupiter 3, is coming in the queue as the next friend, as Jupiter represents knowledge and 7 represents wisdom. Knowledge is always comfortable with wisdom. Next comes number 5, the prince as the friend of Ketu.

Ketu has no non-friends like Prince Mercury. Now let us see who are the neutral planets for Ketu. They are 8,2,9,7. It is understood that 8, 2, and 9 are neutral for 7, but how and why 7 is neutral for 7? The reason is obvious as 7 is headless and it thinks from the heart. Its thinking is illogical then how an illogical thinker can help another illogical thinker? So, it is better to say 7 is neutral to 7 rather than calling them friends.

NUMBER **8**

Now talk about number 8, Saturn. He administers justice for all. He is a judge and never does injustice to anyone. Have you ever seen the justices of a high court and supreme court? How they maintain neutrality, without much involvement in social gatherings and functions.

Planet Mercury, number 5, is his friend. Number 5 is a prince and a small boy, who may not have any work with a judge, which is why 8 has a friend in his step-brother 5. Other friends of 8 are 6,3,7. Numbers 3 and 6 are persons of knowledge as they are councilors to the king. The judge needs their advice for the administration of justice. Ketu thinks from the heart and may not do any mischief, so he is the friend of 8.

Now see these numbers 4*,8*. Relation of 4 and 8 with 8 is friendly when they are occasionally getting together. They are fine in temporary relationships simply as friends. But they may be non-friends if the temporary relationship is further promoted to permanent relationships like marriage, or business partnerships (between 4 & 8, 8 & 8). In simple language, I CAN SAY THAT PERMANENT RELATIONSHIPS CAN'T SURVIVE BETWEEN 8 & 8, 8 & 4, AND 4 & 4.

Now you can anticipate who are the enemy or non-friends of Saturn. The number one enemy is the sun, and the second is number 2. Saturn is the illegitimate child of the sun and the sun can't recognize number 8 as his son, for which he always sees the opportunity to take revenge. Moon is the queen and his stepmother. He considers that due to the beauty of his stepmother, his mother is not recognized as a queen of the sun. Furthermore, if we look from a scientific point of view, the moon is water and Saturn is iron. If both the elements come together iron gets rust. Hence, they are antiplanets, better for them to keep away from each other.

Mars, number 9 is the neutral number for 8.

NUMBER 9

Number 9 is Mars, the commander. He is unpredictable and a fighter planet. Often driven by mood. His friends include 1,5,3. Being given command in the army he is obliged to king. Next comes 5, the prince, the future king. Number 3, Jupiter is the friend of number 9, because he needs advice from the guru.

4 and 2 are non-friends of 9. Rahu is a gangster who can't patch up with the commander. No doubt 2 is queen but 9 doesn't carry out her order. There is a mental war that always runs between the two. More both 4 and 8 are struggling planets.

When comes together make the people struggle, struggle, and struggle.

6,7,8,9 are neutral planets for number 9. How 9 can be neutral for 9. When a commander meets another commander maintain constraint and avoid confrontation. It is the part of discipline that 9, follows, for which 9 is neutral to nine.

Now this is much toward compatibility of numbers. We will know more further in the subsequent chapters.

Chapter.6

LUCKEY AND UNLUCKY NUMBERS

Numbers have a way of taking a man by the hand and leading him down the path of reason. – Pythagoras

Welcome to this new chapter. I hope you have understood the previous chapter on the compatibility of numbers. Unless you understand the compatibility of numbers or the relationship between numbers, you may not proceed to your destination. **The foundation of numerology is based on the compatibility of the numbers.**

Now proceed further to see the lucky and unlucky numbers. Do you believe lucky and unlucky numbers are there? Do you believe in luck or fortune? If luck is not there why the term is coined? Why some people are treated as lucky and some not? Why it is called fortune favor the brave? If the words are there, these words are in our belief system. It may be a myth or reality. If you believe it is unrealistic then it is unrealistic. If you believe yes luck matters, then it is fine. Everything depends on your willpower and belief system. If you ask me about the reality of the lucky and unlucky numbers, I can say yes, it is person-specific. The number which is lucky for you may not be lucky for me and answer is there in the numeroscope. Some people consider their date of birth as a lucky number. But it may or may not be true.

For example, the date of birth of A is 19th June 1968. Now some people conclude that the lucky number of A is 19, 10,1, 28. However, it is not cent percent correct. Unless you find out the moolanka and bhagyanka number and their compatibility, you may not be 100% sure.

Now again visit the compatibility of the number chart for reference.

No	Friends	Non-Friends	Neutral
1	9,2,5,3,6,1	8	4,7
2	1,5,3,2	8,4,9	6,7
3	1,5,3,2,7*	6	4,8,9,7*
4	7,1,5,6,4*,8*	4*,8*,2,9	3
5	1,2,3,6,5	....	7,8,9,4
6	1,5,7,6	3	8,9,2,4

7	4,6,1,3,5	....	8,2,9,7
8	5,6,3,7,4*,8*	(4*,8*,)1,2,	9
9	1,5,3	4,2	6,7,8,9

Now I will try to make you understand with an example. Let us consider the date of birth of **A is 19th June 1968.** In case of determination of lucky and unlucky numbers, only moolanka and bhagyanka numbers are needed. Now in this instance case,

- Moolanka is 1(1+9)
- Bhagyanka is 4 (1+9+6+1+9+6+8)

Now we have moolanka 1 and bhagyanka 4.

Let us see which numbers are friends to 1 and 4. In the friend list of the moolanka (1)- 9,2,5,3,6,1 are present. Can you confidently say which are lucky numbers for A? You can't say because you have seen the partial truth, which is always destructive.

"Half a truth is often a great lie." - Benjamin Franklin

We have not yet seen the friendly numbers of bhagyanka 4. Let us see who is on the friends list of bhagyanka 4. These numbers 7,1,5,6,4*, and 8* are included in the friend's list of number 4.

Now to find out the lucky number we have to select the common friends of both 1 and 4. I can see the common friends of both the numbers are **1, 5, & 6.** Now see who are neutral numbers. In the case of 1, I can see 4,7 as the neutral number. 4 & 7 are present as friends for bhagyanka 4. You can consider 4 and 7 as lucky numbers for A. However, 4 can't be considered as a lucky number because (4=Rahu) it is a slow planet. Similarly, 7 (Ketu) is headless, and may not be fortunate enough for the purpose.

After all the above discussions, you are sure that the lucky numbers of the birth chart of A are 1, 5, & 6.

Now let us search for the unlucky numbers of A.

- Unlucky /unfriendly/bad number for 1 is 8
- Unlucky/unfriendly/bad number for 4 is 4*,8*,2,9

Earlier I have discussed the importance of star-marked numbers, when they will behave as friends, and when as enemies. In conclusion, I may say 2, 8, & 9 are unfriendly or unlucky numbers for the birth chart of A.

Let us take another example to find out the lucky and unlucky numbers of a date of birth. **Consider the date of birth of B is 21.5.2013.**

- ✓ Moolanka of B is 3(2+1)

- ✓ Bhagyanka of B is 5 (2+1+5+2+1+3)

Now,

- ✓ Friendly number or friends of 3 are 1,5,3,2,7*

- ✓ Friendly number or friends of 5 are 1,2,3,6,5

- ✓ Neutral numbers of 3 are 4,8,9,7*

- ✓ Neutral numbers of 5 are 7,8,9,4

From the above friends list we found that 1,2,3,5 are common friends. From the neutral numbers, we found that 4,8,7 & 9 are common. In the neutral numbers, 4,8 is slow and inauspicious, hence not considered as good. Number 7 is headless and may not be auspicious. Only 9 can be considered a lucky number for 3 and 5.

In conclusion, we may say the lucky numbers for the birth chart of B, are 1,2,3,5, and 9. The unlucky/bad number is 6(because 6 is an unfriendly number of 3 and 5 has no non-friend).

How can you use the lucky numbers in your favor?

Let us conclude that you can find out the correct lucky number from any date of birth. Then tell me when, how, and where you can use the number for your benefit. Yes, you can use it as the total number of,

- Number plate of your vehicle.

- House number.

- Mobile number.

- Bank account number.

Now I can show you how to select **the lucky number for B**. His lucky numbers are 1,2,3,5 and 9.

Mobile Number

- 9437258422(9+4+3+7+2+5+8+4+2+2)46=4+6=1)

- 9870823544(9+8+7+0+8+2+3+5+4+4)50= 5+0=5)

Number Plate

- OD4A-4532(4+5+3+2=14) =5

- DL6F-9464 (9+4+6+4=23) =5

- DL6H 9191 (9+1+9+1) =2

In such cases, only digits are considered not the alphabets.

Plot no/Flat No

- ✓ 1324, all the digit calculated together comes to 1+3+2+4=10=1

- ✓ A/14, in such a case A is the flat block number and flat no is 14=5(1+4)

- ✓ 16/12, in this case, 16 is block no, and 12 is plot no. 12 is added together and comes to 3.

Now you get the lucky mobile no, number plate, and plot no/flat no of B. Further, you can select your favorite hotel room from available vacant rooms whenever you visit for any tour out of your city. If you have any option to attend an interview, or join duty then you can definitely select a perfect date that confirms your lucky number.

Hope you are now capable enough to find out the lucky number and unlucky number of any birth chart. Further to get confidence calculate a few birth charts of your friends, family members, and relatives to predict the lucky numbers and unlucky numbers.

Chapter.7

CHARACTERISTICS OF NUMBERS

"Numerology is the bridge between who you are now and who you have the potential to be."– Anonymous

What do you mean by the characteristics of numbers? For example, when we talk about a person, we say he is good and intelligent but proud. He often demands respect but doesn't command it. However, he is a good soul, helps the poor whenever he is approached, etc. Now what do you understand about the man from the above descriptions? These are the qualities of that person, called his characteristics. Some are good and some are not good. As every human being bears some qualities good and bad, every planet also bears some bad and good qualities. As you know every number from 1 to 9 represents nine planets, the presence of the numbers in the birth chart exhibits those characters of the planets.

Let us begin now. When we talk about the characteristics of numbers, it is about the CHARACTERISTICS OF THE MOOLANKA NUMBER of a numeroscope nothing more.

1.

Number one represents the sun, the king of the numbers. Can you calculate how do we find number 1? Can you guess it? Yes, you are right. It comes from, 1, 10,19, & 28. (1+0=1, 1+9=10=1,2+8=10=1). Although the sum of all the numbers is the same, they can have exhibited a little bit different quality. In numerology, they can be divided into three categories.

Category-A: 19. Number 1 is most comfortable with 9. Number 1 is king (Sun) and 9 Mars is commander. When both are best friends, the kingdom can witness progress and prosperity. That is why it is placed in such a category. (You can find their relationships in the chapter on the compatibility of numbers.

Category B: 1 & 10. Both 1 and 10 are kings. They can provide support if needed. So placed in this category B.

Category C: 28. Here 1 comes with the combination of 2 and 8. 2 is the moon and 8 is Saturn. Both don't like each other's company. Further moon represents water and Saturn iron. When comes together they react chemically and rust results. This is why 28 is placed in the category C bracket.

CHARACTERISTICS

Number 1 is the number of the sun. The people with moolanka 1 can have the following characteristics;

- They are born leaders. They often rise to the highest rank and file even if started small. They may be the leader of a team, pressure group, organization, etc. Politics may suit them. But don't like petty politics.

- They are high-minded. They can find their own path, for which they are the pioneer. They are hardworking people.

- They are authoritative and command respect for their work and activities.

- They are boss. Administrations suit them much. They are perfectionist and dominating. They don't allow other people to rule over them.

- They are resilient people. They believe setbacks are temporary and stepping stones for success. Never accept defeat as a permanent feature.

- They can become good politician, and leaders and do good in government departments.

- They can become good entrepreneurs.

- They are faithful and royal like lions.

- They are egoistic, rigid, and stubborn at some point in time.

- They are prestige conscious and asking for help for their own purpose is difficult.

Overall, people with moolanka 1 are royal, pioneer, hardworking, leader, and authoritative. They believe in perfection.

All the above features can be seen in 1, 10, 19, and 28. But in the case of 19, they are more successful than other numbers. Let me give you some real-time examples here;

Mukesh Ambani, (19/04) the chairman of Reliance Industries, the Indian Billionaire is ruled by number 19. He got the fortune from his father Dhirubhai Ambani (28/12) and made the company toward further glory. His father ruled by 28, struggled in his initial days, and founded Reliance Industries. More famous people born with 1 as a moolanka, are Slim Helu (28/1), Bill Gates (28/10) Ratan Tata (28/12), India Gandhi (19/9), Susmita Sen (19/11), Aishwarya Rai (1/11), Elon Musk (28/6), etc.

2.

Number 2 represents the moon, given the status of queen. How can you get the number 2 from the date of birth? It can be 2, 11, 20, and 29. These numbers can be simply divided into A, B, and C categories.

A category: 11. 2 comes from 11 called the master number. 1 represents king/sun. 11 means the power of two kings, which is why in this category.

B category: 2 and 20. 2 is standing alone without any support or struggle.

C categories: 29. It is a combination of 2 and 9. Moon doesn't like the company of Mars. They are nonfriends.

CHARACTERISTICS

You have seen the moon. How pleasant and beautiful is it? But it grows in the bright fortnight or WAXING PHASE of the moon (Shukla Paksha) for 15 days and diminishes in the dark fortnight or WANING PHASE of the moon (Krishna Paksha) for 15 days. It means the people of Moolanka 2 are

94

not constant in mind. They sometimes behave like an immature child. Now we can say, they are;

- Indecisive in their actions and behave like immature chap.

- They are good-looking, soft-hearted, and attractive.

- They are good planner but at the same time very lazy.

- They always compromise things when things turn ugly in relationships.

- They are blessed with sensitivity, kindness, and harmony but these people often suffer from mood swings.

- There is every apprehension for them to go into depression, making their lives difficult.

- They are very cooperative and supportive. They also need support for their growth.

- They are feminine characters and love and feel comfort in the company of females.

- They are good healer, social workers, and councilors.

- They are diplomats, mediators, and love a peaceful environment.

- They can work for the best customer satisfaction.

In conclusion, I can say Moolanka 2, are good soul. They are soft-spoken, gentle, diplomat, and look attractive. They need support and provide support.

However, there is a twist to the number 29. **The people born on the 29th of any month may witness marriage issues. If married without a matching birth chart may face difficulties in married life.** However, it is not a universal conclusion. It depends on other numbers also in the chart.

Famous people with 2 as Moolanka are Shah Rukh Khan, (2/11) Amitav Bachchan (11/10), and Rajesh Khanna (29/12), etc.

3.

Number 3, is Jupiter, the Guru of gods. He is pious in his approach and attitude. Let us see how can we find 3. It can be 3, 12, 21, and 30. All four numbers can be categorized into A, B, and C.

Category A: 12. It is the strongest combination of king and queen. Here the king is in the Moolanka's seat.

Category B: 21. 12 and 21 look the same but the difference is visible. In 21, the queen is in the driver's seat. 2 can't be compared with 1. It is a weaker combination than 12.

Category C:3 and 30. 3 and 30 are sitting alone without any support from anywhere.

CHARACTERISTICS

Let us see the characteristics of number 3.

- ✓ People of Moolanka 3 are driven by knowledge. They always need to be knowledgeable and hungry for it. Sometimes they prefer knowledge to money.

- ✓ They are creative people and innovative in their thought processes.

- ✓ They are problem solvers and optimistic people.

- ✓ THEY THINK OUTSIDE THE BOX and have a unique approach to day-to-day life issues.

- ✓ They can imagine and visualize things better.

- ✓ They may be good at art, literature and music.

- ✓ The teaching profession may suit them better.

- ✓ They can also do well in administration, police, bank, politics, salesmen, and technology.

- ✓ They are spiritual at their heart.

- ✓ They may be religious in practice in daily life.

- ✓ They love mystic science and occult.

- ✓ They focus on accomplishment and success.

- ✓ They are good communicators and very good at public speaking.

In conclusion, I can suggest that **the people ruled by Moolanka 3, should never touch liquor and eat non-vegetarian food.**

Overall, these people are the powerhouse of knowledge and good soul. You can ask them for advice to solve any issues relating to personal importance. They can be educated, religious, and spiritually minded. Occult professions can be best suited to them. Examples of famous personalities, born with Moolanka 3 are Rajinikanth (12/12), Govinda (21/12), Kareena Kapoor Khan (21/9), Rani Mukerji (21/3), Yuvraj Singh ((12/12), etc.

4.

Number 4 represents Rahu. We can get 4 from the date of birth of 4, 13, 22 and 31. Now we can categorize them into the following categories.

Category A: 22. It is a magic number like 11.

Category B:31. Combination of Jupiter and the sun are good as they are friends.

Category C:4. It is standing alone and nobody is there to uplift or support 4.

Category D:13. You may be surprised to see its inclusion in the worst category. A combination of 1 and 3 is good, one is king and another is his councilor. But in this case, it is not true.

13 IS A KARMIC NUMBER AND IS TREATED AS INAUSPICIOUS. But why? Because it has a debt and sin of the previous incarnations. In Europe and many Western countries, there is no lane no 13. In many cities houses or flats, no 13 are not given due to this belief of karmic number. At the end of MYAN CALENDER's 13th Bakun was superstitiously feared as a harbinger of the apocalyptic 2012 phenomenon. The fear of number 13 has a specifically recognized phobia,

triskaidekaphobia, a word first recorded in 1911. **Further, 4 is associated with death for Cantonese-speaking Chinese people.**

CHARACTERISTICS of 4

- ✓ The people having Moolanka 4 are rowdy and rebellious. They need to follow their own rules and independent character.

- ✓ They are energetic, knowledgeable, clever, and confident.

- ✓ They are born with leadership qualities and diligence.

- ✓ They love discipline, act in it, and want others to obey it

- ✓ They are logical people. They believe in logic and remain in search of logic in everything. They can't believe anything without logic.

- ✓ They are confidential and secretive. You may believe them undoubtedly.

- ✓ They are short-tempered and argumentative. They get angry for simple things.

✓ They are also abusive and use vulgar language to anyone.

✓ They are impulsive and sometimes encouraging and motivating.

✓ They are good planners.

✓ Best-suited career for them in project management, accounting, engineering, and organizing units.

People with Moolanka 4 are disciplined, rebellious, secretive, logical, impulsive, and simultaneously abusive. IN MANDARIN, THE NUMBER 4 IS PRONOUNCED AS "SI", WHICH SOUNDS SIMILAR TO THE WORD DEATH. It is due to superstition connected with the number 4.

5.

Number 5, is the number of Mercury, the prince. In the Lo-Shu grid, you can find it positioned at the center of all the numbers. It gives balance to the life. We can find the number 5 from the date of birth of 5, 14, and 23. We can include them in 3 categories.

Category A: 14. 14 is a combination of 1 and 4. It is an ANGEL NUMBER, that signifies positivity and spirituality. Sun and Rahu's combination represents creativity, communication, and adaptability.

Category B:23. The Moon and Jupiter combination is good. Both support each other.

Category C: 5. It stands alone, hence placed as the C category.

CHARACTERISTICS 5

- ✓ People with 5 as a Moolanka enjoy a very peaceful and balanced life. They know how to balance and manage finance, life, and relationships.

- ✓ They take responsibility for their own life and are accountable for up and downs of their lives. They never like interference in their lives.

- ✓ They are lazy people and never prefer physical labor and exercise. They may be fat due to good eating habits and lack of physical exercise. However, many things depend on the Bhagyanka also.

- ✓ They are romantic people and love their partner much. They are young at heart and self-loving. They are very careful about themselves.

- ✓ They are successful people. They can excel in their professional and personal life.

- ✓ They can be good writers and can excel in marketing and travel agencies.

- ✓ They can be good entrepreneurs.

- ✓ The people with 5 Moolanka are lucky because they have no non-friends or enemies.

- ✓ They are resilient people and often bounce back smartly.

- ✓ They are talkative and sometimes become chatterboxes.

- ✓ They are independent and desire to find fresh solutions to problems.

- ✓ They are social and find connections with others. However, their impatience can sometimes lead to conflicts.

- ✓ They are good communicators and adapt to any situation.

Overall, people of number 5 are romantic, self-cared, accountable, and blessed. They are born to success. Jawaharlal Nehru (14/11), William Shakespeare (23/4), Dr. S. Radha Krishnan (14/11), Albert Einstein (14/3), Edward VII (23/6), etc. are examples of a few famous personalities born on the earth with 5 as their Moolanka.

6.

Let us talk about Venus, the number 6. You know Venus as the councilor of demons. We can get 6 from the date of birth 6, 15, and 24. Let me put them in three different categories as done for the other numbers.

Category A+, 15: Earlier you have seen that we have put the combinations of different numbers into a, b, c, and d categories. But here we put 15 in the A+ category. You may ask, why so elevated status? The reason is simple it is a combination of father-son, a king, and a future king. Both are very comfortable with each other.

Category B, 6: Here 6 may be alone but he is sufficient to influence others.

Category C, 24: Here 2 is queen and 4 is gangster. A combination of both is not comfortable. They are non-friends.

CHARACTERISTICS of 6

The people having 6 as their Moolanka exhibit the following characteristics.

- ✓ They are romantic people. They love to enjoy life. Prefer to live in luxury and glamor.

- ✓ They are manipulative. Often resort to lying. But they present the lie as a fact. You can't detect them lying.

- ✓ They are diplomatic and intelligent. Manage things properly and responsibly.

- ✓ They love sex and like to tour and travel.

- ✓ They are also family men, love their children much, and are cared for by their children.

- ✓ They are trustworthy, sympathetic, and gentle.

- ✓ Professions like hospitality(hotel), teaching, and health care, nursing(doctors) can suit them.

- ✓ They can do well in social service.

- ✓ They can excel in music and acting professions.

- ✓ They should not marry Moolanka numbers 2,3, and 9.

In conclusion, I may say they are loving, romantic, and manipulative. Manage things diplomatically. They are family men.

However, there is an apprehension of marriage-related issues in the case of females, if 6 is coming from 24. It is observed that in such a case female creates the issues. But nothing to worry about, every problem has a solution. For example, **Sri Aurobindo (15/8) and the Dalai Lama (6/7) are born with 6 as psychic numbers.**

7.

Who is 7? Guess it. You are right it is Ketu the headless thinker planet. We can get the number from 7, 16, & 25. Now put them into different categories.

Category A, 16: In this combination king is power and 6 is knowledge. When knowledge is acted together with power makes wonder. Further, 6 is a symbol of luxury and a king can promote it and enjoy it. That is why 16 is in the A category.

Category B,25: It is a mother and son combination. A queen and prince combination. This combination is good as it bears no responsibilities.

Category C, 7: Here 7 is alone with a good heart and wisdom.

CHARACTERISTICS of 7

The people with the number 7 as Moolanka may have the following characteristics.

- ✓ They are the people of Golden Heart. They think from the heart not from the head, as Ketu is headless.

- ✓ They are very simple and believe everything is truth without thinking of its logical conclusion.

- ✓ They are highly educated and do research in different fields.

- ✓ They are betrayed in love due to their simplicity.

- ✓ They are spiritual people of the religious band of minds.

- ✓ Occult profession is most suited to them. They can earn name, fame, and money if chosen as a profession.

- ✓ They may be good in education if opted for a career.

- ✓ Health, research, philosophy, and, psychology, sectors may suit them.

- ✓ Marriage life may not be so smooth.

Number 7 is a symbol of disappointment. The people may be disappointed in love life, money, health, and marriage.

Rabindranath Tagore (7/5), Sir C.V Raman (7/11), Issac Newton (25/12), Marie Curie (7/11), and AB Vajpayee (25/12) are noted figures of the world born on Moolanka as 7.

8.

Let us see number 8, Saturn, the lord of karma or justice. We can get the number 8 from the date 8,17, & 26. Let them be included in different categories.

Category, A 17: It is a good combination of 1 and 7. 7 gets the head of a king. Now he is complete and behaves like a benevolent king.

Category B, 8: It is 8 alone and acts independently.

Category C, 26: It is a combination of beauty and luxury. You may say it is a good combination. But it is not true. 2 is the moon and queen of God, 6 is Venus, the councilor of demons. 2 is not comfortable with 6. Number 6, has no issue with the queen but the moon is not comfortable with Venus.

CHARACTERISTICS OF 8

You know that number 8, is a number of struggles. Saturn is a slow planet. We have discussed it in the compatibility of numbers, in the previous chapter. The people born with 8 as the Moolanka are normally struggling in life. If you talk about the order of struggles, I may say the struggle can increase from 17,8, and 26 respectively. In fact, the struggle is the benchmark for this number and nothing can be owned easily without effort. The characteristics of 8 may include;

- ✓ They are likely to struggle in life. May not get anything easily.

- ✓ Everything gets delayed in their lives. The work that is supposed to be completed today can be completed tomorrow.

- ✓ They are hardworking and industrious. They are resilient and can achieve anything.

- ✓ They are task-oriented and committed. Unless the task is complete, they never relax.

- ✓ They are good orator and good at heart. They look like task master but at the same time very understanding.

- ✓ They believe in their efforts and qualities of work. It is very difficult to convince them.

- ✓ They are down-to-earth people. Understands others very well.

- ✓ The law sector is the most suited profession for them.

- ✓ They are born to lead and the money market can suit them best. CEO and high-powered executives are best for them.

- ✓ THEY THINK THEY ARE THE BEST AND MOST AMBITIOUS.

- ✓ They are super disciplined with a smile on their face.

- ✓ They are natural leaders and sources of inspiration for others.

- ✓ **They love for money**(legal) and may forget the most important things like friendships and relaxation.

It is observed that women with 8 as a Moolanka may struggle in their marriage life. They may not get a suitable life partner or if married conjugal life mayn't be so successful. They may face problems during pregnancy.

110

Narendra Modi (17/9), AB DeVilliers (17/2), and Asha Bhosle ((8/9) are a few examples of famous personalities born with 8 as their Moolanka.

9.

Now we are at last number 9. Nine represents the planet Mars. Mars is a warrior, a commander. We can get 9, from the date, 9, 18, 27. As usual, these numbers can be categorized as follows,

Category A, 9: A warrior/commander is sufficient to protect himself and others.

Category B, 27: A combination of 2 and 7 is not a good combination. 2 is moon and 7 is Ketu. Both are enemies to each other. Similarly, 2 as a queen never liked the company of a Ketu, a headless.

Category D, 18: It is interesting. Why 18 is placed in the D category in place of C? Because 1 and 8 are antiplanet. Nature is different and is an enemy of each other.

CHARACTERISTICS OF 9

- They are MOOD-DRIVEN PEOPLE and never compromise with their principles.

- They are egoistic people and prefer death to loss/compromise.

- They are disciplined. They can be most suited to the ARMY, AND POLICE.

- They are **unpredictable characters.**

- They are spiritual leaders, compassionate and humanitarian pursuits.

- They believe in idealism and desire to make a meaningful difference in the world.

- They are DONOR LIKE THE MYTHICAL HERO KARNA.

- Son and father relations very deteriorating. IF A MALE HAS A DATE OF BIRTH OF 18, YOU CAN BLINDLY SAY FATHER-SON RELATIONSHIPS ARE AT A LOW LEVEL. The son doesn't want to see the face of his father. You may be shocked by these predictions, but are there any solutions? If the son is in the study, put him in the hostel. Never do business jointly. Avoid staying together under the same roof.

- They may have lost their father before they were born or during childhood.

People of Moolanka 9 are disciplined, mood-driven, egoistic, compassionate, humanitarian, and unpredictable character.

112

Saint Ramakrishna Paramahamsa (18/2), Leo Tolstoy (9/9), Donald Bradman (27/8), Martina Navratilova (18/10), Bruce Lee (27/11), Nelson Mandela (18/7) are a few examples born with 9 as Moolanka.

Now this much for this chapter. I hope you understand it well and can use it for the purpose most suited for you. You may be excited to know its veracity of characteristics. It is a good sign that you are interested in numerology. Collect some dates of birth of your friends and relatives and find out the secrets hiding behind them. Let us go through the next chapter.

113

Chapter.8

81 COMBINATIONS OF MOOLANKA AND BHAGYANKA

"Numerology recognizes that numbers are vibrations, and each vibration is different from the next..." - David A. Phillips

Welcome to this most fascinating chapter to understand the combination of Moolanka and Bhagyanka. In earlier chapter 3, you learned how to calculate the Moolanka, Bhagyanka, and Kua number. You also have enough knowledge of how to prepare the numeroscope. If you are not convergent in preparing a Numeroscope, then nothing to worry about. Be determined to learn and have a positive attitude to change and learn. Educate yourself.

"There is no end to education. It is not that you reach a point where you can say, "My education is complete." - Ralph Waldo Emerson

This chapter is very very important for the calculation of your future and taking follow-up actions. Imagine that the Moolanka and Bhagyanka are two horses drawing your life chariot. The speed as well as safety drive of your life chariot depends on the capabilities, speed, health, training, and eating habits of your horses. If your horses are good friends with each other, then your life is easy, and can achieve anything you desire to get. In its reverse, you are destined to suffer. 81 combinations of Moolanka and Bhagyanka can give you a clear picture of your future prospects and if required remedial measures for the purpose can be prescribed. We shall try to give some star rating to the combinations out of 5 stars. Now see what is there for you in the combinations.

ONE AND ITS COMBINATIONS.

M	B	Ratings
1	1	★★★★
1	2	★★★1/2
1	3	★★★1/2
1	4	★★★
1	5	★★★★
1	6	★★★1/2
1	7	★★1/2
1	8	(-)?
1	9	★★★★★

The above rating is based on their relationships with each other. You can get an overall idea from the above table.

EXPLANATIONS OF THE ABOVE COMBINATIONS.

<u>1-1combination:</u> Both are royal and give respect to each other and work together. Both are powerful and support to each other. Given 4-star rating. 1 represents the Sun, the king of the solar system, and in numeroscope. King represents power and authority. Where power and authority are there in front and at the rear. This person is destined to succeed in professional life. They are king-like and lucky.

<u>1-2Combination:</u> One is king and another is queen. They cooperate and respect each other. 3 and half star rating. 1 and 2 combinations are considered very good. It is a combination of king and queen. They are successful in their professional and personal life. Dairy, water-related professions can suit them. You can opt for a bright career in the Navy.

<u>1-3 Combination:</u> One is king and another is Jupiter, the councilor. Three and a half-star rating. It is an auspicious combination that can give name, fame, and money. In a horoscope, if the sun is placed with Jupiter in a house is considered auspicious. The people are knowledgeable and powerful. You can say as

successful in real life. Teaching, coaching, and counseling may suit them much.

<u>1-4</u>   Combination: King and gangster combination. Three-star rating. This combination is good for jobs like public relations, banking, and politics. Personal life is good. They may witness some family problems unless they understand each other. In money matters, 1 should be guided by 4. Understanding is a big point in this combination.

<u>1-5 Combination:</u> King and Mercury, the prince, the future king, a good combination. Four-star rating. This combination is one of the best in numerology. The people with such a combination are born to success in every field. This is a combination of father-son. Combination of power, authority, and knowledge. They can perform best in the financial sector, administration, and politics.

<u>1-6 Combination:</u> King and Venus, the councilor. Three-star rating. It is a combination of power, knowledge, and glamour. The people of this combination can be attracted to glamour, media attention, and happiness. They can perform better in film industries, hospitality sectors, behind-the-camera, songs and music, tours, and travel. They can run liquor shops, bars, casinos, etc. to make a huge success.

<u>1 & 7 Combination:</u> King with Ketu, is not a good match. Two and a half-star rating. Not a bad

combination. The people of such combination riches with wisdom. Can perform well in education, teaching, occult, etc. They are also good at research and spiritualism.

<u>1& 8 Combination:</u> King(sun) and Saturn, anti-planets. Hence the rating is negative. It is a combination of the Sun and Saturn. It is an anti-combination. Imagine a chariot being run by two horses from both front and back sides. What would happen? I am not comfortable saying that this is a struggling combination in respect of health, finance, success, and relationships. People with such a combination can face challenges in their marriage lives. But nothing to worry we have tools to eradicate the negativity. You can find the solutions in my next books.

<u>1 & 9 combination:</u> King and Mars, the best combination, deserve a 5-star rating. The best combination in numerology. The people with such a combination are super successful. If you are not successful, the problem is there in your Numeroscope and most probably in your name spelling.

THE NUMBER 2 AND ITS COMBINATIONS

M	B	Ratings
2	1	★★★1/2
2	2	★★
2	3	★★1/2
2	4	★1/2
2	5	★★★
2	6	★★1/2
2	7	★ ★ (★★★★)
2	8	(-)
2	9	★1/2

LET ME DISCUSS IN DETAIL THE NUMBER 2 AND ITS COMBINATIONS.

<u>2-1 Combination:</u> It is a good combination. Here queen is the Moolanka and the king is the Bhagyanka and deserves a 3 and ½ star rating. It is a combination of the moon and the sun. People of this combination get success but they struggle in their early days.

<u>2-2 Combination:</u> Here the moon is the Moolanka and Bhagyanka both. It is not so bad combination and deserves a 2-star rating. The moon and moon combination are good but their minds are not

mature. They sometimes behave like children. They can be successful in water and milk-related business. The Navy can suit them. Service in Water plants, dairy, ice factories, bottling plants, and related businesses can suit them better.

<u>2-3 Combination</u>: It is the moon and Jupiter together to run your life's vehicle. Deserve 2 and ½ star rating. Not a bad combination. People with this combination can try their luck in the teaching profession, education sectors and can achieve success in the occult profession.

<u>2-4 Combination:</u> Moon and Rahu combination is not treated well. Hence treated with one and ½ star rating. Moon with Rahu is not a good combination. People with such a combination can struggle in their professional and personal lives. There is every possibility that they may undergo depression in their lives at least once if not given remedies earlier.

<u>2-5 Combination:</u> This combination is good. It deserves 3-star ratings. Moon and Mercury are a good combination. The people influenced by such a combination can be successful in their lives. They may succeed in the real estate, banking, and financial sectors.

<u>2-6 combination:</u> It is a combination of moon and Venus. It's not a bad combination deserving 2 and 1/2-star ratings. Moon may not be comfortable with Venus but later is comfortable with the moon. Due to the influence of Venus

people can get luxury, comfort, and pleasure in their lives. The world of glamour can suit them. Sweet business can suit this combination. Fashion, media, tour, and travel are other sectors in which they can excel.

<u>2-7 Combination:</u> It is a combination of moon and Ketu. This combination can be average and at the same time may be excellent for which a 2/4-star rating is given. This combination is treated as average. Moon and Ketu are struggling in combination. But the people coming under such a combination can do wonders if they prefer to research, and professions like numerology, astrology, occult science, card reading, and mystic science. Basically, THESE PEOPLE CAN BE SUCCESSFUL IN ANY FIELD OF RESEARCH.

<u>2-8 Combination:</u> This combination is not desirable, which is why negative ratings. It is a moon and Saturn combination. The moon represents water and Saturn represents iron. This combination is a symbol of struggle in personal and professional lives. **Health is a matter of concern for the people coming under this combination.** But remedies are there for the above problems in numerology.

<u>2-9 Combination:</u> The combination of the moon and Mars gets one and ½ star rating. This is not considered a good combination. Moon and Mars are a struggling combination. People of this combination struggle in their lives. **Their**

marriage and conjugal lives may be a bigger issue in their lives.

THREE AND ITS COMBINATIONS

M	B	Ratings
3	1	★★★
3	2	★★1/2
3	3	★★★
3	4	★★1/2
3	5	★★★
3	6	(-)?
3	7	★★1/2/★★★★
3	8	★★
3	9	★★

<u>3-1 combination</u>: This is a combination of Jupiter and the Sun, considered good. The people coming under such a combination are successful people. They can excel in education, healing, occult, and coaching sectors including politics.

<u>3-2 combination</u>: It is a good combination. People coming under the influence of such a combination can do better in teaching and healing professions. They are also good at dairy and water treatment, and bottling plants.

<u>3-3 combination:</u> This combination represents Jupiter and Jupiter. THE PEOPLE OF THIS COMBINATION SHOULD NEVER TOUCH NON-VEGETARIAN FOODS AND ALCOHOL. Maintain a very honest lifestyle. People are intelligent and are successful in the teaching profession. Occult science and stationery article business may suit them. Being knowledgeable they try to do so many things at a time. **They are considered good starters and bad finishers**.

<u>3-4 combination:</u> This is a combination of Jupiter and Rahu. Being a Dev-Guru, Jupiter is respected by Rahu. But Rahu may not get such type of respect from Jupiter. The people of such a combination can do better in sales and marketing. Law sectors like the judiciary and legal consultancies may suit them.

<u>3-5 combination:</u> It is a good combination. One is Guru and another is a prince. Guru is a powerhouse of knowledge and the prince is the seeker of the same. Both have respect for each other. **The people with such a beautiful combination are outstanding orators and good communicators**. They can be good writers and can do well behind the camera. Journalism and the banking sector may suit them as professions.

<u>3-6 combination:</u> This is one of the worst combinations. Remember, I have asked you to imagine a chariot drawn by two horses opposite

to each other. Can that chariot move further? The answer is very clear. If you need to go in the chariot, remove one horse. It is only one solution. The success of people coming under the 3-6 combination is bound to suffer in their personal lives, professions, and health. **The marriage lives may be alarming**. But, don't be disappointed, we have solutions for the same and you can find the solutions in my next books. The teaching and occult science profession may suit them.

<u>3-7 combination</u>: This is an auspicious combination. Knowledge and wisdom come together. The people coming under this combination are successful people. In terms of knowledge and wisdom, they deserve 4-star ratings but in terms of success got 2.5 stars. They are highly educated. **Research, education sector, and administration like IAS and other State Administrative Services may be suitable for them**. The occult science may be the best-suited profession for the people of such a combination.

<u>3-8 combination:</u> This combination is not so good, rather not so bad. The people of such a combination can struggle due to 8. Education and law sectors may suit them. The printing press can be a good profession for them as both 3 & 8 represent the printing press.

<u>3-9 combination:</u> This combination is not bad but the success rate is 40%. The people with such a combination can do better in education, police, army, and military services.

FOUR AND ITS COMBINATIONS

M	B	Ratings
4	1	★★★1/2
4	2	★★
4	3	★★1/2
4	4	★1/2
4	5	★★★
4	6	★★★
4	7	★★★★
4	8	★1/2
4	9	★

Number 4 represents Rahu. He is treated as a good gangster. The above ratings indicate his relationships with other numbers. Let's discuss each combination for better understanding.

4-1 combination is given a 3 and half-star rating. One is a gangster and another is a king. Here 4 has little to do with a powerful king. People with a 4-1 combination can be successful in their lives.

They can become good traders and business tycoons. Politics can also suit them well.

4-2 combination is not good. Rahu can eclipse the moon once or more times in a year. It indicates that people of this combination can suffer from depression in their lives. Marriage life may witness some issues. Water and milk-related businesses can suit them.

4-3 combination is the combination of Rahu and Jupiter. It is neither a good nor a bad combination. The people coming under such a combination can do well in the teaching and education sectors.

4-4 combination is a very low rating. Why? Can you imagine its reason? You can't say two gangsters can stay together forever. Permanent relationships such as marriage, and business between two 4 is difficult. A simple relationship like hi-hello, and how are you is good for them. 4 is considered a slow number. People coming under 4-4 are very slow in their progress and achievements. They can do better in sales marketing and law.

4-5 combination is treated as good. The people ruled by this combination are successful in their lives. The sectors like media, law, banking, politics, and finance can suit them the best.

4-6 combination is a very good combination. Both Rahu and Venus share the same nature and are good friends. Both have tamasika prakriti/ nature. If you are coming under this combination, should do well in the media, hotel, beauty Parlor, spa and saloon, law, and liquor business. Bars and restaurants can give you big business. You can do business with any luxury brand like cosmetics, vanity bags, and ladies' items.

4-7 combination is a very good one. Here 4 is the head and 7 is the tail of a complete body. Rahu got its body and Ketu its head. If wisdom is applied wisely then the people of such a combination can succeed. But success may come late but definitely gets. Occult professions like Vastu, numerology, healing, angel card readings, and politics can be profitable for them.

4-8 combination is not good. Both are slow planets. The people of 4-8 combination struggle in their lives. The expected result may not come in proper time. Law, police, and army may be good professions for them.

4-9 combination speaks about struggle. 9 represents Mars, which means bloodshed and surgery. **People of such a combination should be careful about their health. They may face accidents. They may visit their doctors regularly**. They may get success in their lives in professions like police and the army.

FIVE AND ITS COMBINATIONS

M	B	Ratings
5	1	★★★★
5	2	★★★1/2
5	3	★★★
5	4	★★★
5	5	★★★★
5	6	★★★1/2(★★★★1/2)
5	7	★★★
5	8	★★★
5	9	★★★

See the above chart. What you have observed? High rating points against every combination. The rating indicates that the success rate for every combination is not less than 60%. Why such high ratings? Remember I told you that Mercury is a prince with no enemy. If you have no enemies, your performance and relationships will definitely be high.

5-1 combination is one of the best combinations. It is a combination of mercury-sun, known as *budhaditya Yoga* in astrology. It is an auspicious combination, which gives success in life to the persons coming under such combinations.

5-2 is the combination of mercury and moon combination, son-mother combination. The people of this combination can earn name, fame, and money from an early age. They are successful in real estate and property.

5-3 is a good combination. The people of such a combination, ARE GOOD COMMUNICATORS. They can preset the things attractively. Teaching, public relations, journalism, and banking sectors are most suited for them.

5-4 combination is also good for the people coming under such a combination. They are successful but may be late a little bit due to number 4. But success is definitely there.

5-5 combination is good for success and fulfillment. But number 5 people are lazy. When 5-5 combined their laziness increases. They are often fatty but responsible. They have the knowledge and intelligence for which they can complete 6 hours of work in 4 hours. How do they make a difference?

Let me tell you a story, which can fit the nature of a 5-5 combination.

Jonson was engaged as a woodcutter in a factory without any progress for the last 6 years. Now the organization hired Sheru for the same job as Jonson. Within 2 years Sheru was given a higher package and rank, which made Jonson complain with the authority. Authority replied, "Yes his performance and output are much more than you. Develop your skill and you will get the higher package" Now Jonson tried hard to cut more trees per day but failed. To find out the solution he decided to meet Sheru to know the secret. Sheru told him that he cut trees for one hour and then took a break TO SHARPEN THE AXE.

Sheru is coming under number 5. Now you all understand why the people of such a combination do much work in less time.

5-6 combination is a symbol of success. 5 represents balance and 6 number is the symbol of luxury. The people of such a combination can be successful in the star hotel business, finance, media houses, pubs, casinos, liquor business, etc. Tours and travel may be a good option for them.

5-7 is also a good combination. Here Ketu got the head of Mercury. Knowledge and wisdom are used constructively. The people of such a combination can perform well in the fields of research, occult, computer science, robotics, finance, banking, and education sectors.

5-8 combination is good as both are brothers and sons of the king, the sun. They have no enmity between them. The people of such a combination do exceptionally well in real estate and property, agriculture, farming, horticulture, etc. Because both 5 and 8 are earth elements.

5-9 combination is fine for an **administrative job**. The people of this combination can do well in banking and teaching professions also. They may fit in the armed forces as administrative officers.

SIX AND ITS COMBINATIONS

Six is a symbol of Venus. This number gives us the name, fame, money, luxury, glamor, and reasons for celebrations.

M	B	Ratings
6	1	★★★ 1/2
6	2	★★ 1/2
6	3	(–)?
6	4	★★★
6	5	★★★★/★★★★★
6	6	★★★
6	7	★★★ 1/2
6	8	★★★
6	9	★★★

<u>6-1 combination:</u> This is a combination of Venus and the Sun, the councilor and the king. It is a very good combination. The people coming under this combination are successful and good leaders. They are good in politics, luxury hotels and

restaurants, liquor, and other GLAMOROUS BUSINESSES.

<u>6-2 combination:</u> This combination is not bad. The people of such a combination can be good poets. The sweet business may suit them well.

<u>6-3 combination:</u> It is not a good combination but the worst one. There is a clash of interests between 6 & 3. 6 is Venus, the Guru of Demon whereas 3 Jupiter is the Guru of Gods. Both are considered anti and struggling combinations. The people of such a combination suffer in their lives. **They may be successful in their lives but health and marriage life may be questionable**. For example, Jayalalitha (24.02.1948) former chief minister of Tamil Nadu.

6-4 combination: It is a good combination. Here the mentor of the demon is Venus and Rahu is a demon gangster. Rahu can be guided by Venus. The people of this combination can be successful in the police and army. The glamour, marketing, etc. world also suits them.

<u>6-5 combination:</u> It is an outstanding combination. 6 represents money, glamour, name, and fame, abundance, and 5 represents the balance in life. This combination does wonders in the lives of the people coming under such a combination. They are destined to achieve success in their lives. If they are not getting the success, then some mystery is there in his/her

name spelling. The business is associated with luxury, glamour, literature, hotels, finance, restaurants, media, etc. can suit them.

<u>6-6 combination:</u> This combination is good. The glamour is the focus of this combination. The people of this combination can be the best poet. Because Venus is the best poet as declared by Krishna in Bhagavad Gita. (munīnām apy aham vyāsaḥ kavīnām uśhanā kaviḥ)/ Ushanas means Shukracharya or Venus). They can be good actors, dancers, directors, producers, news anchors, makeup artists, playback singers, beauty advisors, dieticians, graphic designers, etc. They can open businesses like spas and saloons, pubs, hotels, luxury brands, etc.

<u>6-7 combination:</u> Where knowledge and wisdom meet together that is 6-7 combination. Both are Guru-Sishya, mentor and mentee. Physical sports may suit the people coming under this combination. Sports like cricket, football, hockey, basketball, baseball, and lone tennis are the fewer of them. They may also test their luck in the research, luxury, and glamour world.

<u>6-8 combination:</u> 8 is Saturn, the judge, who needs luxury in life. The people coming under these types of combinations are righteous and judgemental. Both luxury and law sectors can suit them.

<u>6-9 combination:</u> It is not a good combination but 60% success rate. Mars is a warrior but saint-like

character. The people of such a combination can have names, fame, and money, but CONTROVERSIES WILL FOLLOW THEM. The professions like police, doctor(surgery), and military services can suit them.

7 AND ITS COMBINATIONS

Number 7 is Ketu, the headless planet. It is called *Chhaya Graha* or shadow planet. Most of its performances depend on its combination.

M	B	Ratings
7	1	★★★
7	2	★ ★ ★ (★★★★)
7	3	★ ★ ★ (★★★★)
7	4	★★★★
7	5	★★★
7	6	★★★★
7	7	★ 1/2
7	8	★★
7	9	★★

<u>7-1 combination:</u> It is a good combination, as number 1, the sun is the head of Ketu. The people coming under the combination can get success in their lives. The occult and teaching are considered the best profession for the people of such a combination. They can be good as writers

and politicians. For example, former chief minister of Odisha Naveen Patnaik (16/10/19460) rules Odisha for 24 years at a stake.

7-2 combination: It is given a 3-star rating for the combination. Knowledge and intuitions when come together work toward success. But, when they prefer to work in occult science, they can excel, for which given 4-star ratings.

7-3 combination: It is a combination of wisdom and knowledge. Given a 3-star rating for this combination, means the success rate is 60%. However, when the people of such a combination work in the fields of spiritualism, research, occult, healing, card reading, angel healing, and the teaching profession, the success rate becomes 80% and gets a 4-star rating.

7-4 combination: This combination is good because Rahu and Ketu get their original form. They can be successful in leadership. Can work in NGOs, training, mentoring, and occult professions.

7-5 combination: It is a good combination for success and money. They can be successful in computer applications, like graphics design, editing, sales and services, and banking and financial sectors.

7-6 combination: It is a very good combination. It is a combination of Sukrachrya/ Venus and his disciple Ketu. Here brain of the combination is Venus. The people of such a combination can be good sportsmen, good poets, and perform well in the occult.

<u>7-7 combination:</u> It is not a good combination. It is like a combination of a blind picking the hand of another blind to cross the busy road. The people of such a combination may be good friends but may not help each other. THEY ARE MORE LIKELY TO BE FRUSTRATED IN THEIR LOVE LIVES. THEY ARE OFTEN CHEATED FINANCIALLY AND EMOTIONALLY BY THE OPPOSITE SEX. THEY CAN HAVE EXTRA OR PREMARITAL AFFAIRS. They are more attracted to the opposite sex.

<u>7-8 combination:</u> It is not so bad combination. But the people of such a combination can experience delays in every work in their lives. Occult, teaching, and law professions can suit them.

<u>7-9 combination:</u> This combination's rating comes to 2 stars, which means the success rate is 40%. It is an average combination. The people coming under such a combination can do well in occult, teaching, and army services.

Now let's discuss the next combination 8.

NUMBER 8 AND ITS COMBINATIONS

M	B	Ratings
8	1	(-)?
8	2	(-)?
8	3	★★
8	4	★
8	5	★★★
8	6	★★★
8	7	★★
8	8	★
8	9	★

The rating chart is ready for your observations. What do you observe now? The ratings are very low in comparison to other tables. The reason is known to you. If you are not able to recall the reason for the time being. It is not an issue. I am here to tell you. Because the 8 number is Saturn, which moves very slowly. It is a struggling planet for the numeroscope. The life prospects depend heavily on the Bhagyanka.

8-1 combination is the worst. It is a combination of antiplanets. Both are non-friends. The people of such a combination struggle much in jobs, business, and relationships. There is a question mark about their marriage and couple's lives.

8-2 combination is equally bad as an 8-1. It is a combination of moon/water and Saturn/iron.

The people coming under this combination are destined to suffer in personal, professional, and married life. **Health may be one of the areas to be worried about**.

8-3 combination is good with a 60% success rate. The people of such a combination can do well in law, judiciary, real estate, and the teaching profession. Married life may suffer. The printing press may be a good option for this type of combination.

8-4 is a bad combination. The people coming under such a combination are bound to suffer. Work may not progress as expected. Jobs in the pharma and automobile sectors can be suitable for them. Permanent relationships with the people of this combination (8-4, 4-8) are to be avoided.

8-5 combination is good. Both are brothers. The people of this combination are very successful in their personal or professional lives. Land, property, real estate, banking, and leather are best-suited sectors for them.

8-6 combination is good. The people of this combination can have a success rate of 60% in their lives. They can get jobs in hotel industries, law sectors, and judiciary.

8-7 combination is not so bad. The people of this combination can do better in public sector banks, metal industries, occult, teaching, and law sectors.

8-8 is one of the least preferred combinations. This is a struggling combination, but **physical labor can earn a name and fame.** Sectors like law, judiciary, shoe business, and leather business can suit the people of 8-8 combination. But they can struggle in permanent relationships like marriage, and business partnerships. They can do better in outdoor sports like tennis, football, cricket, etc. For example, Roger Federer (8.8.1981), the former tennis star of Switzerland.

8-9 combination is considered ok. One is a judge and another is a commander. Both are disciplined and can get success in life but can have some delay. The people of this combination are powerful, rowdy, and command respect. Defence and laws are the best-suited sectors for them.

9 AND ITS COMBINATIONS

Number 9 is pious but commander. He can influence the other partners. But it is an unpredictable number. The people coming under number 9 as Bhagyanka may behave like this.

M	B	Ratings
9	1	★★★★
9	2	★★
9	3	★★1/2
9	4	★1/2
9	5	★★★
9	6	★★
9	7	★★
9	8	★★
9	9	★

9-1 is a good combination. It is a combination of the king and the commander. Number 9 is unpredictable. The people coming under this combination can be successful in their professional lives. However, the actual profession can be detected from the birth chart. Job in armed forces, and surgery can suit them.

9-2 is not a good combination. Characters of both 9 & 2 are more or less opposite. One is a disciplined soldier and another is a beautiful queen. There is a clash of interests between them. The people coming under the 9-2 combination are sad people. **Their family lives are disturbed. The couple often quarrel with each other. The establishment of peace**

between them is short-lived. If not married getting married is also a big issue.

9-3 combination is not bad. It is the combination of advisor to the king and the commander of the king. Commander needs the advice of Jupiter on some occasions. Teaching, healing, and jobs in the armed forces can be suitable for the people of 9-3 combination.

9-4 is a combination of disappointment. Because both are non-friends. The people of such a combination struggle in their professional and personal lives. **They are prone to accident. Health is a subject of concern for these people.**

9-5 is a good combination, as both are friends. It is the combination of a commander and a future king. Further, 5 is the number of balances. The people coming under this combination are successful in their personal and professional lives. The finance and banking sectors can be better for them to flourish. They can go for technology, medicine, defense, etc.

9-6 is not a good combination. 9 & 6 are nonfriends. One is saint-like and another is fond of glamour, pleasure, and enjoyment. The people of such a combination can have money, power, name, and fame but **may have a scandal. They may not enjoy peaceful conjugal lives. Marriage may be an issue in their lives.** For example, Salman Khan (27.12.1965) famous Bollywood actor and producer.

9-7 combination is manageable. As Ketu is headless, he accepts the head of Mars. The people of this combination can be successful in their personal and professional lives. Healing, teaching, surgery(doctors), and occult may be good professions for them.

9-8 combination is not bad, as both are neither friends nor foes. The people of such a combination can be good lawyers, armed forces officers, and police.

9-9 combination is one of the worst. The people of such a combination believe in discipline and simplicity. They are saint-like. **They never like to get married. Suppose married never enjoy sexual pleasure.** They may have very strong physics. Jobs in the army, and police can suit these types of people.

The above combinations and the probable professions are indicative. The actual predictions can be made after going through the entire Numeroscope.

Chapter.9

KUA NUMBER AND ITS IMPORTANCE

"Numbers are the universal language offered by the deity to humans as confirmation of the truth." – St. Augustine

You have heard the name of Kua number. But are you excited to know why such terminology is given? Kua is referred to as Pa Kua. Pa means "eight" and Kua means "trigram". Now the complete meaning of Pa Kua is an eight-sided octagon symbol with a Trigram on each side. These trigrams represent different aspects of the universe and energy flow. But for our convenience, we use it as a Kua number. It is of Chinese origin. Pa Kua is also an ancient Chinese martial arts tradition practiced by young and old for fitness, health, and well-being. However, Your KUA NUMBER, also called MING GUA, is a personal number calculated from your date of birth and gender. It's based on the Eight Aspirations Theory within Feng Shui.

Many have a question in their mind why Kua numbers for males and females is different for the same date of birth? **The reason is that Feng Shui philosophy is deeply rooted in the concept of YIN and YANG, representing opposing yet complementary forces in the**

universe. Males are traditionally associated with **YANG ENERGY** (active, dynamic), while females are associated with **YIN ENERGY** (receptive, nurturing). During the preparation of the numeroscope, the Kua number creates phenomenal differences in the birth chart and its outcome. It creates magic on many occasions.

METHODS OF CALCULATION OF KUA NUMBERS

For example, take a date of birth as **13.02. 1969.** It can be different for a male and a female.

Male: Make a total of all the digits of the date of birth such as 1+3+2+1+9+6+9= 31, and now reduce 31 into a single digit by adding the number, 3+1=4. Now subtract this number from 11. 11-4=7. Now we have the Kua number of a male from the above date of birth, which is **7.**

Female: For the female you have to add 4 with the total date of birth we calculated above. Now add 4 to 4. Now, the total of the digit 4+4(8) comes to 8. Now we got the Kua number of a female as **8.**

WHEN DOES IT MAKE A DIFFERENCE?

Why this formula is used for the calculation of the Kua number is a mystery. It is believed that this formula was given by Saint La-Shu to numerology. As we follow many mathematical and scientific formulas without asking any questions, in numerology we follow the same metrics.

Now let's calculate some Kua numbers.

For example, take an imaginary date of birth as 19.09.1968. For males let's calculate the Kua number first. **1+9+9+1+9+6+8=43=4+3 =7.** The next step is **11-7=5.** Here we get 5 as Kua number. In this date of birth 5 was missing. Now its placing in the Lo-Shu grid gives strength and balance to the birth chart.

Now calculate the Kua number of a female from the same date of birth. Kua number shall be **7+4=11=1+1=2.** Again, what do you observe here? Number 2 is added to the chart which was missing. I have told you earlier that every number has its importance in numerology, especially when it forms any Yoga in **Numeroscope**. It can be Raj Yoga or completing any line.

You know we have nine single-digit numbers in numerology. From your date of birth, we find three numbers, such as Moolanka / PSYCHIC NUMBER, Bhagyanka / DESTINY NUMBER, and Kua number. So far, the weightage of the number is concerned, the Moolanka is given 75%, the Bhagyanka comes next at 50%, and Kua at 25%. However, on some occasions, the Kua number steals the show, as noted in the above example of a male.

★ ● ✪ ● ★

Chapter.10

MASTER DESTINY NUMBER

"Numerology is the study of the mystical significance that numbers hold. Numbers have a way of transcending beyond mere symbols for counting and can reveal deep truths about our lives and the universe."
— Anonymous

Some numbers in our date of birth are treated separately. If you ask why, the answer may not be with anyone. You may say it has been accepted as such for a long without giving any valid reason. However, it has effects on the date of birth.

In numerology, digits like 11, 22, and 33 are called **master destiny numbers**. It is not easy to know the master destiny number by adding the total digit as we normally do to find out the Bhagyanka.

For example, take a date of birth of **12.2.2013.** let's add all the digits 1+2+2+2+1+3=11. Now we get 11 as the bhagyanka. Can we further add 1+1 to get 2 as the bhagyanka or 11 as the master destiny number? To find out the destiny number we have to add the total digits in vertical order, as follows;

12

+02

+2013

=2027=2+2+7=11(2)

Yes, it is a master destiny number.

Now take another example, of DOB, **11.01.1979**

Add all the digits 1+1+1+1+9+7+9=29=11(2)

Is the above-calculated number 11 being master destiny number?

Let's add them vertically to know the reality.

11

+01

+1979

=1991=1+9+9+1=20=2

No, it is not a master destiny number.

Now take an example for the determination of 22 as master destiny number.

Date of birth **12.12.1942**

Now additions of the above total digits come to 1+2+1+2+1+9+4+2=22. Is it a master destiny number? Let's calculate to know the facts.

12

+12

+1942

=1966

=1+9+6+6=22(2+2=4)

Yes, 22 is a master destiny number.

If we find the master destiny number as 11 or 22, we are supposed to predict the future trend based on 11 or 22 not as 2(1+1) or 4(2+2). Let me prepare a chart on the above date of birth for your better convenience. DOB-12.12.1942(male)

44	9	222
3		7
	111	

M-3, B-22(4), K-7

In the case of master destiny/bhagyanka, you have to predict on 11/22, not on 2/4.

148

MASTER DESTINY NUMBER 11

Characteristics:

The people coming under Destiny Number 11 exhibit certain unique characteristics. Such as,

> They are big dreamers and not doers. They dream big without any follow-up actions.

> Set unrealistic goals and challenges. Unrealistic goals are bound to give unrealistic end results.

> But they can be dowers and excellent performers. How? If guided and supported by a backup or support system. The support system may include family, friends, mentors, etc.

MASTER DESTINY NUMBER 22

Characteristics:

The people of master destiny number 22 are

> Dreamers and doers.

> They set the realistic goals to achieve.

> They prepare the road map to achieve the goals.

> They are resilient people.

> They are disciplined.

> Good starter and a fine finisher.

Why? Because 4 comes from adding 2+2. 4 is the symbol of discipline, organization, leadership, and knowledge. Although 4 is treated as a number of struggles, here it is the most successful.

MASTER DESTINY NUMBER 33

The master destiny number 33 has not been seen yet.

Characteristics;

- Unconditional love

- Work for Humanity

- Spiritual and preacher.

In conclusion, I am to say that the master destiny number plays a crucial role in an individual's life and its calculation is separate from normal calculation.

Chapter.11

KARMIC NUMBER

"In numerology, every number has a certain power which is expressed both by its symbol to denote its representation and by its connection with the universal principles." — David A. Phillips

In numerology, karmic numbers are linked to the philosophy of karma. It is a concept that our actions have positive and negative consequences. These consequences can carry over into future lifetimes. The karmic theory says humans undergo different incarnations based on past experiences.

Karmic debt numbers, are believed to indicate areas where you may have made mistakes or imbalances in past lives. They show up in your current life as challenges or lessons to be learned. It further indicates that you may not run away from the assigned duties entrusted to you by infinite intelligence.

Karma is a core concept in Dharmic religions like Hinduism, Jainism, and Buddhism, which originated in the East. Karmic debt numbers specifically tied to past lives and karma are less prevalent in traditional Western belief systems.

However, the concept of karmic debt numbers is a more recent adaptation within Western numerology, influenced by Eastern traditions.

There are four main karmic debt numbers: **13, 14, 16, and 19**. Each number carries its own specific meaning and potential challenges.

Here's a brief overview:

<u>Karmic Number 13:</u>

This number indicates that the people coming under this number HAVE NEGLECTED THEIR ASSIGNED DUTIES in previous lives. It indicates a need to focus on hard work and discipline to achieve success. People with this number may struggle with feelings of insecurity or a lack of foundation.

<u>Karmic Number 14:</u>

This number shows the ABUSE OF FREEDOM by the people in their previous incarnations. It suggests a need to develop freedom and independence in a healthy way. Never try to grapple with rebellion or misuse of freedom in this life to repay the debt.

<u>Karmic Number 16:</u>

This number indicates THE ABUSE OF LOVE in previous lives. It is about finding a balance between materialism and spirituality. People with 16 as a karmic debt number may have been **overly focused on material gain in past**

lives. Now they need to learn the importance of spiritualism for growth and fulfillment in this life.

<u>Karmic Number 19:</u>

This number indicates the ABUSE OF POWERS in previous lives. This number is related to learning humanitarianism and service to others. People with 19 as a karmic debt number may have been selfish or self-centered in past lives. Now they need to develop compassion and generosity to get rid of karmic numbers.

It's important to remember that karmic debt numbers aren't meant to be a burden. Instead, they are seen as opportunities for growth and personal development. By understanding the challenges associated with your KARMIC DEBT NUMBER, you can work toward overcoming them and achieving a more balanced and fulfilling life.

What do you understand now? Are you coming under the karmic debt account? If yes, it is your time to rectify your actions. If you undermine the influences of the numbers you may suffer. Remember you have to be debt free in this incarnation.

Not everyone has a karmic debt number. These numbers only appear in certain calculations based on your birthdate or name.

CONCLUSION

As we finish our journey through numerology, it's clear that this practice is more than just numbers. It's a powerful tool for self-discovery and understanding the world. We've covered a lot, from the origins of numerology to its various systems, giving you a solid base to appreciate its depth.

We started by introducing numerology and its basics. Then, we explored its history and different methods, including the interesting Lo-Shu Grid. We looked at how numerology can be used in lotteries and the unique concept of the Numeroscope.

We also learned about ancient principles and how they affect our lives. We examined how numbers can improve relationships and which ones bring luck or challenges. By understanding the characteristics of numbers, we gained insight into personality traits and life paths.

We explored number combinations to understand their dynamics. Learning about the Kua Number showed us how our environment and well-being are influenced by numerology. Lastly, we discussed the Master Destiny Number and the Karmic Number, and their impact on our life's purpose.

As you close this book, I hope you feel empowered to use numerology to unlock your destiny. Whether you're seeking personal growth, better relationships, or a deeper understanding of the universe, numerology offers a unique and powerful path. Thank you for joining me on this wonderful journey. May the insights you've gained lead you to a life of greater clarity, harmony, and fulfillment.

DISCLAIMER

The information provided in this book, "**Unlock Your Destiny with Numerology,**" is intended for educational and entertainment purposes only. Numerology is a fascinating and ancient practice that many people find valuable and insightful. However, it is important to remember that numerology is not a science and should not be relied upon as a sole means of making significant life decisions.

The content of this book reflects the author's personal views and interpretations of numerology. While every effort has been made to ensure accuracy, the author and publisher do not guarantee the completeness, reliability, or suitability of the information contained within. Readers are encouraged to use their own judgment and consider seeking advice from professionals when making decisions related to health, finance, relationships, or other areas of their lives.

By reading this book, you acknowledge and agree that the author and publisher are not responsible or liable for any actions taken based on the information provided. Numerology should be approached with an open mind and a sense of curiosity, recognizing that its insights are just one of many tools that can offer guidance and self-reflection.

★ ● ✪ ● ★

MAY I ASK YOU FOR A SMALL FAVOR?

At the outset, I want to give a big thanks for taking out time to read this book. You could have chosen any other book, but you chose mine, and I totally appreciate this.

I hope you got at least a few actionable insights that will have a positive impact on your day-to-day life.

Can I ask for 30 seconds more of your time?

I would love it if you could leave a review about the book. Reviews may not matter to big-name authors; but they're a tremendous help for authors like me, who don't have many followers. They help me grow my readership by encouraging folks to take a chance on my books.

To put it straight, reviews are the lifeblood of any author. I feel this book **"UNLOCK YOUR DESTINY WITH NUMEROLOGY"** shall enrich you with some actionable steps.

Please leave your review by visiting the **"Review Section "** of this book's page on this platform.

It will just take less than a minute of your time, but will tremendously help me to reach out to more people, so please leave your review.

Thanks for your support of my work. And I would love to see your review.

158